CW01460265

Werner Herzog

Memoir

The Art of Embracing the Abyss

CONTENT

Chapter 1: STARS, THE SEA

The lamentations ended around midday. Some of the women yelled and tore their hair. When they left, I went to look for myself. It was a modest stone building near the cemetery at Hora Sfakion, a village on Crete's south coast with only a few cottages spread across the high cliffs. I was sixteen. The small chapel had an aperture but no door. In the half-dark interior, I noticed two corpses so near together that they were touching. Both were guys. Later, I learned that they had slain each other in the night; in that isolated, archaic area of the world, they still practised vendetta, or blood retribution. All I can recall now is the man's face on the right. The colour was lavender blue with yellow splotches. Two large blood-soaked cotton wool pads emerged from the nose. He had been shot in the chest with a round of buckshot.

At nightfall, I headed out to sea. I worked on a fishing boat for a few nights, maybe on the few dark nights before and after the new moon. One boat hauled six lampades, or skiffs, out to sea, each carrying one man. We were all dumped several hundred yards apart and left to drift. The sea was as shiny and smooth as silk, with no waves. There is an enormous quiet. Each boat featured a large carbide lantern that shone down into the abyss. The lamp attracted fish, particularly cuttlefish. They had an unusual fishing method. A small shining piece of wax paper roughly the size and shape of a cigarette was attached to the end of a fishing line. This attracted the cuttlefish, who grabbed the booty with their tentacles. To assist them hold on, the bait was attached to a wire wreath. You had to know exactly how deep down the lure was beneath the surface because the moment the cuttlefish felt themselves being drawn up into the air, they would immediately release their loot and return to the sea. You had to speed the remaining arm's length of line to swing the cuttlefish onto your boat.

The first few hours were spent in silence, waiting for the lamp's artificial moon to take effect. Above me was the orb of the universe, stars that I felt I could reach up and hold; everything was rocking me in an unending cradle. And below me, lit vividly by the carbide lamp, was the depth of the ocean, as if the firmament's dome had formed a sphere around it. Instead of stars, there were many flashing silvery fish. Bedded in an incomparable cosmos, above, below, and all about, a deafening silence, I found myself startled. I was certain that I had learned everything there was to know. My fate was revealed to me. And I knew that after one such night, I'd never be able to get older. I was certain I would never see my seventeenth birthday because, as lit up with grace as I was now, there could never be anything like regular time for me again.

Chapter 2: EL ALAMEIN

Some time ago, I came upon a postcard from my mother dated September 6, 1942, and written in pencil. The stamp depicting Adolf Hitler was preprinted. The postmark reads clearly: Munich, the movement's centre. The postcard is addressed to Herr Professor Dr. R. Herzog and Family of Grosshesselohe, near Munich. To my grandfather, Rudolf Herzog, the family patriarch. My mother decided not to inform my father.

I was born soon before the turning point of World War II. In the East, the German Wehrmacht was laying siege to Stalingrad, which would lead to a devastating German defeat within months, while in North Africa, General Rommel was attempting to push through to El Alamein, which would soon lead to a similar disaster for the so-called Thousand-Year Reich. Much later, when I was twenty-three and needed to leave the United States quickly because I had violated the terms of my visa and was about to be expatriated back to Germany, I fled to Mexico, where I had to find a method to earn a livelihood. I worked as an arena clown in charreadas, a Mexican style of rodeo, riding on young bullocks despite never having ridden a horse before. My chosen sobriquet was El Alamein, because no one could pronounce my full name and instead referred to me as el Aleman, or the German. I, on the other hand, insisted on El Alamein because, much to the delight of the fans, I was brutally beaten at every appearance, a subtle homage to the German defeat in the North African desert. Every Saturday, this defeat, and, more specifically, the injuries I always sustained, could be marvelled at again.

My forefathers were prominent administrators and officers, and my grandfather, whom I never met because he died when my mother was eighteen, was a major on the Habsburg general staff. According to her recollections, he enjoyed surreal humour and the absurd. For two years, he was stationed in Üsküp (modern-day Skopje) and wore only one glove. Later, in a café in Vienna, he removed both gloves in front of a waitress, and to everyone's surprise, he had one hand thoroughly browned and the other as white as snow. The Croatian side of my family had nationalist views and backed Croatia's independence from the Austro-Hungarian Dual Monarchy. Such affinities ultimately led to fascism. With Hitler's help, a populist leader, known as a poglavnik, seized control in Croatia for three years until the war finished, and that was the end of it.

My grandmother was from a respectable household in Vienna; my mother was never particularly close to her since she had never valued respectability. I only knew my grandma from a few trips; the one that stands out is when I went to see her with my mother near the end of her life, in a home. My grandma was perplexed and asked for a glass of water, which I retrieved for her from the sink. "Such a delicacy," she continued, taking tiny sips and thanking me repeatedly for something so delicious.

I began doing this while still in high school since I needed money for my first film productions. Perhaps out of insecurity, because I had failed to propose to her before leaving, she married my cousin without alerting me while I was in the States. When I returned, she had just returned from her honeymoon and had run away with me for a few days, but neither she nor I had the resolve to change history. She didn't want to go directly back to her husband, my cousin, so I took her back to her parents, who were waiting for me with her four brothers. Perhaps there were only three; in my memory, they have been elevated to a position of vast superiority. I was not going to just drop my lover at her parents' door; I was well prepared to confront them. Her brothers, big Bavarian lunks who all played ice hockey, had threatened to murder me if I revealed my identity. To this day, I am confident that there was no physical contact, but I still had a swollen cheekbone, as if I had been hit hard. It wasn't until four decades later, at a family birthday, that I had another brief interaction with him, but we were never close again, despite our mutual wish to be.

Following this, my lover from before my first trip to the United States appeared to be cursed later in life. She kept drawing misfortune. She had two children with my cousin, but their marriage ended. Her subsequent relationships likewise went poorly. Finally, she plunged to her death from the Grosshesselohe Bridge. In vintage photos of us together, we always appear completely calm, with no hint of the impending disaster. I'm still disappointed with myself for abandoning her throughout my time in the States without having the fortitude to tell her. Women have always played a dramatic role in my life, no doubt because there were strong emotions involved. But I never quite understood the immense mystery and sorrow of love. My connections were almost never superficial. I was driven by the monster of love, yet without women, my existence would have been nothing. Sometimes I picture a world without women. It would be uncomfortable, destitute, and like sliding from one void to another. But I was lucky in love, perhaps more than I deserved.

My great-great-grandmother's recollections date from 1829. She grew up in East Prussia. "My dear little girl," she writes to her grandchild, my grandmother, "when I sent you a letter this summer with recollections of our old home, you wrote to say you would like it if I wrote down some of the stories I told you about my youth. My earliest conscious memory stems from my third year. I believe the year was 1829. I seem to envision myself in our drawing room at Schloss Gilgenberg. My mother, whose features are no longer visible to me, is sitting on a chair at her sewing table, busy with some handicraft in a window niche; the windows were some distance off the ground; I clamber up into the niche and then onto the chair; standing behind my mother, in my girlish way, I try to arrange and stroke her hair. Then the day arrives that I seem to see before me still, and that I will never forget: I am in Mother's bedroom, it is morning, she has left her bed and is lying on the sofa, I am playing beside her; there must be someone else in the room as well, because I hear the words: "She's lost consciousness again," and I hear a call for help, the servants come and pick her up and carry her back to bed. Then I hear another request: "Bring a warming pan for her feet." The feet were rubbed and warmed, but it was ineffective; they would not warm up again. It was, as I subsequently learned, the first time she had left her bed since the birth of my baby brother. I recall being called in to examine the stillborn baby.

To me, the Berger farm in Sachrang felt both bucolic and troubled; in my case, this was caused by the Second World War's catastrophes, volatility, and streams of refugees. Before I started school, my brother Till and I were tasked with caring for the Lang farm's cattle. We boys were acquainted with young Eckart Lang, whom we dubbed the Butter because his cruel father regularly forced him to churn butter. Minding the cows provided us with our first paycheck, which was minimal but enhanced our sense of independence. It's even possible that we made money earlier, when we were the same age and carted beer and lemonade up the Geigelstein on the draft pony.

The height difference from Sachrang is around 800 metres, and we were barefoot because we did not wear shoes during the summer. Shoes were only available in the fall and winter until the end of April; in the months without r, May, June, July, and August, we didn't even have underpants under our lederhosen. Today there is a road leading up the mountain, but back then we scampered up a steep trail and arrived in an hour and a quarter. Today's tourists take four hours. A cheese-making family lived near the Alpine meadow, including a young woman named Mari. She was the only one of them who lived up there all year; the tale went that she would never have anything to do with the valley or the people down below because she had once been in love and been abandoned by someone.

Her father had placed her in a rucksack and transported her up the mountain when she was a baby, and she had grown up there. She had only been down to the valley once in her sixty years of adulthood because her signature was required for something, which I believe was pension payments. A few years ago, soon before her death, I met her on the mountain with my younger son, Simon. Despite the fact that she was over ninety, she appeared wild and dishevelled. Most days, young men from the mountain rescue agency peeked in on her from a nearby lodge.

My milking experience came in handy many years later with the astronauts who made up the crew of one of the Space Shuttles. My preoccupation with the unmanned expedition to Jupiter, which was proving extremely challenging and had numerous setbacks, served as a backdrop. The Galileo space probe was finally launched into deep space in 1989, after multiple delays and revisions in plans. To achieve the required velocity, the probe had to be sent around Venus and twice around Earth, with the gravitational attraction of both planets creating a sling effect. The mission lasted fourteen years, and when the probe was nearly out of fuel, NASA decided in 2003 to direct it with the last of its power around one of Jupiter's moons before exposing it to the big planet's gravity. Galileo was sent into Jupiter's gaseous atmosphere to burn up as ultra heated plasma to avoid contaminating the moon (Europa), which is covered in a thick sheet of ice with a supposedly liquid ocean beneath and perhaps forms of microbial life. What struck me the most about this day was how practically everyone was in tears, and how, despite being able to hear the signals from the space probe clearly, the mission was abruptly terminated. Even though signals continued to arrive, it had been planned in advance that the probe would continue communicating for another fifty-two minutes. That was the amount of time the signals from the already-defunct, burnt creature took to arrive on Earth.

This event prompted me to investigate deeper. In an archive, I discovered these beautiful 16 mm recordings made by the astronauts during their Shuttle voyage. I assumed they were the only recordings in that format; the rolls of film were still wrapped in their original lab plastic, and no one had thought to do anything with them. Of course, video footage of the probe's launch in 1989 existed, as did 8 mm film before that, but this particular crew included an astronaut with a special interest and aptitude in film. Other crew members had used the camera, but he was responsible for most of the footage. I mention this man because he made films of amazing beauty that left an indelible impression on me. He had served as a test pilot on all types of US Air Force aircraft and had also led a nuclear submarine.

I instantly concluded that his footage, together with other pictures under the Antarctic ice, would serve as the foundation for my science fiction film The Wild Blue Yonder. Alternatively, it might be utilised to create a story based on its own properties. I wanted the Shuttle astronauts to appear in the film—yes, they were all sixteen years older, but according to my story, they were going at such high speeds that 820 years would have passed in Earth time. Time was distorted. They are about to settle on a depopulated world.

It took several months for me to meet them all at the Johnson Space Center in Houston. When I was introduced, chairs were arranged in a semicircle in a large hall, and the fairly elderly astronauts were sitting on them. I knew they were all great scientists in their own right: one of the two female astronauts was a biochemist, the other a medical doctor, and one of the guys was one of the country's most distinguished plasma physicists—all no-nonsense professionals. I stated that, in fact, I was not a creature of the film industry at all, but rather someone who learned how to milk cows at the end of the war. Even after all these years, I still shudder when I think about the odds, but I went on to tell them that in my work with actors and faces, I could frequently detect some of what lurked beneath.

In Sachrang, we learnt how to tease trout. When trout detect humans, they hide under stones or hang motionless beneath overhanging vegetation on a riverside. However, if you reach for them cautiously with both hands and grab them firmly, you can catch them. Because we were hungry, we would frequently capture one or two in the Prien River on our way to school, cage them in shallow pools, and collect them on our way home. The mother would then fry them in the pan. I can still see them, freshly slain and headless, leaning in the pan. Sometimes they would even bounce around. Our lives were spent primarily outside; even in the dead of winter, our mother would not hesitate to send us out for four hours at a time. As nightfall fell, we'd be standing at the door, gibbering and our garments caked in snow. The door would be pushed open at precisely five o'clock, and our mother would quickly sweep the snow off of us with a twig broom before allowing us inside. She believed fresh air would be beneficial, and we had a fantastic time, especially since there were very few fathers in the area, so everything was anarchic in the best sense. I was relieved that we didn't have a drill sergeant in the house directing us what to do. We discovered it for ourselves, without being informed.

Chapter 3: MYTHICAL FIGURES

Sturm Sepp is a mythological figure from our boyhood. He worked on the Sturm farm next door, and he leaned forward at the hip like a ninety-degree hinge. To us, he was a giant of a man, a relic of some gloomy, incomprehensible past. He had a massive grey shovel beard and an equally large pipe dangling from his mouth. We could tell from his bicycle how tall he would be if he stood straight up. The saddle was so far above the frame that only a giant could reach the pedals from there. Sturm Sepp remained mute. Nobody had ever heard him say a word. On Sunday, at the bar, his mug of beer was brought to him without his having to order it.

One mystery that still haunts me to this day is an aeroplane that spent a long time hovering over the mountain behind the house, as if hunting for something. Then, as we could clearly see, it dropped something shiny and mechanical, possibly aluminium. I can't remember if it was on a parachute or a balloon. It was marked with a flag and appeared to move from one treetop to the next. People down in the valley could see it as well, but because it was already dark, a search party of men did not set out to find it until the following morning. They'd been gone all day, and it was nearly dark when they returned from the mountain. We were all dying to find out what it was, but nobody would tell us. Something intriguing had been discovered, but we were not allowed to know what.

I belong to a generation that may be unique in history. People in generations before mine experienced significant transitions, such as from a European world to the discovery of America or from a craftsman's world to the industrialised period, but each was the result of a single momentous transformation. Despite the fact that I was not a member of an agricultural culture, I was able to watch and experience how fields were mown by hand with scythes, how grass was turned, how hay wagons drawn by horses were loaded with large two-tined hay forks, and how the hay was brought into the barn. In mediaeval times, young men were treated as serfs. Then, for the first time, I saw a machine—still drawn by a horse—that spun and hurled hay into the air with two horizontal prongs; I saw the first tractor, and, to my surprise, the first milking machine. This marked the move to machine farming. Then, much later, I witnessed industrial farming taking place in the huge expanses of the American Midwest, where massive combine harvesters drove in formation across fields that stretched for miles. Nobody bothered these monsters, even though each still had a human driver. However, they were digitally connected; each cockpit had many computer screens; and steering was done automatically via GPS, allowing for precisely straight lines.

I have witnessed similar shifts in the field of communication since ancient times. I had no understanding of movies. I had no idea such a thing existed until one day, a man with a mobile projector approached us in our one-room village school in Sachrang and showed us a few films, which completely failed to impress me. There was no telephone in the village, and I made my first phone call when I was seventeen. Televisions were just introduced in the 1960s; in Munich, we first saw the news or a soccer game at the janitor's flat a level above ours. I witnessed the dawn of the digital age, the internet, with content selected for me not by humans but by algorithms. I've received emails from robots. Even though I don't use social media, it has fundamentally altered all kinds of communication. Video games, surveillance, AI—there has never been such a cluster of profound developments in human history, and I cannot conceive that future generations will encounter such density of change in a single human lifetime.

I have witnessed similar shifts in the field of communication since ancient times. I had no understanding of movies. I had no idea such a thing existed until one day, a man with a mobile projector approached us in our one-room village school in Sachrang and showed us a few films, which completely failed to impress me. There was no telephone in the village, and I made my first phone call when I was seventeen. Televisions were just introduced in the 1960s; in Munich, we first saw the news or a soccer game at the janitor's flat a level above ours. I witnessed the dawn of the digital age, the internet, with content selected for me not by humans but by algorithms. I've received emails from robots. Even though I don't use social media, it has fundamentally altered all kinds of communication. Video games, surveillance, AI—there has never been such a cluster of profound developments in human history, and I cannot conceive that future generations will encounter such density of change in a single human lifetime.

Poverty was widespread, and it didn't strike us as remarkable except in exceptional cases. Children from poor upland farms located higher up the valley attended the local school, which had four classes taught simultaneously in one room. One of them, Hautzen Louis, was consistently late every day. I believe he had to work in the cowsheds at home before it became light, which always made him late. In the winter, he came bombing down the hill on a sleigh, and he was always covered in snow from head to foot.

Seventy years later, I encountered Fräulein Hupfauer at a class reunion in Sachrang. She had a different surname because she had married and widowed in the interim. Despite her advanced age, she remained warm and passionate. She had always thought that when I was in her care, I would lead a remarkable life; my mother reiterated this to me countless times after I had grown up. And yet, nothing in my childhood indicated anything remarkable, save perhaps in the negative. I was quiet, restrained, and prone to sudden outbreaks of fury; in general, I posed a threat to everyone around me. I was capable of silent brooding, for example, since I wanted to know why six times five equaled five times six. It even appeared to be a general theory, as eleven by fourteen was equal to fourteen by eleven. A few years ago, I met Roger Penrose, arguably the greatest living mathematician, and asked him how he worked, whether using abstract algebraic methods or visualising the problem. He informed me it was purely through visualisation.

I brought myself under control by practising strict self-discipline. To this day, pure discipline defines a large portion of my character. But there is still a gruff, often jockey palling between Till and me, which occasionally confuses outside onlookers about our continuous familiarity. A few years ago, we attended a family reunion on the Spanish coast, where my brother was residing at the time. We spent a fantastic evening at a seafood restaurant, thanks to his offer and expense. My brother sat behind me and wrapped his arm around me as I scanned the menu. Something began to smoke, and I felt a light prick on my back before realising that he had set fire to my shirt with his cigarette lighter. I ripped it off, and everyone was shocked, but the two of us laughed loudly at a joke that no one else found funny. Someone lent me a T-shirt for the rest of the evening, and the small hurting spot on my back was soothed with a glass of prosecco.

Chapter 4: FLYING

I've longed to fly since I was very small. Not on an aeroplane, but by myself, with only my body and no gear. We were put on skis as babies, although the Sachrang valley has no slopes worthy of the term. So we started ski jumping, created our own ramps, and had some fantastic crashes. On one such fall, my brother landed with the tips of his skis drilled so deeply into the snow that they were stuck, and he had to remove both of his boots. Without skis or boots, he plummeted down the remaining distance. Rainer, a neighbour, and I tested out another ramp outside the hamlet. It appeared big to us at the time, but today it appears tiny and insignificant. We hoped to one day become world champions and rented decent jumping skis. They turned out to be more than seven feet long, miles longer than we were, and they were also wide, with five rills grooved into the underside to keep the ski on track as it went down the ramp. This one had a natural approach, as it was a natural slope rather than an artificially created tower. Right at the top was a large pine tree that you could lean against at a 90-degree angle to the ramp before pushing off into the icy dual tracks of the fall. My friend had the most awful mishap. I was standing on the slope beneath the ramp, watching him leap into the tracks. But he didn't get the skis properly within them, and there was no way to halt on the treacherous descent. I can see him as if it were today, battling all the way down the slope to get his skis into the tracks. But he fell headlong into the woods. There were a few rocks as well. The sound of the impact still shakes me. I found him with horrendous brain injuries that were too severe for me to convey. I was convinced that he was either dead or about to die. He attempted to talk, but the impact had knocked out all of his molars. It took long, agonising minutes for him to lose consciousness, but he eventually did. I was torn between running to the village for help and abandoning him alone, or staying by his side despite the fact that there was nothing I could do to help. I ultimately opted to carry him, despite the fact that he weighed more than me. It was a pretty steep descent to the landing place. I was lucky, or rather he was, since a farmer arrived with a pony and sleigh. My friend was taken to the hospital, where he remained in a coma for three weeks or less until waking up and recovering. He suffered no substantial long-term harm, except that the majority of his molars had to be replaced with silver dentures. Furthermore, he has always had headaches whenever the weather changed. Decades later, after we had entirely lost contact, there was a strange sign of life from him. The ZDF sports show Sportschau, which aired highlights from German soccer league games, included a feature called "Goal of the Month." It must have been the early 1980s; in any case, the goal chosen and played again in the show was determined by which of the short-listed contenders was chosen by the greatest number of fans who wrote in on postcards. A studio star chose one card from among two hundred thousand, and the happy winner received a free trip and two tickets to the next Germany game. The postcards were laid out in large mail bags in a semicircle on the studio floor, and the guest reached into one to pluck out a card. The name of the lucky winner was announced: Rainer Steckowski, Sachrang. The statistical improbability is so stunning that no one will believe me, but I recall the incident. Rainer's accident ended my dreams of ramps and flying. It was several years before I wanted to go near a ski jump again.

In 1981, Erstes Fernsehen presented a breaking news special report from Cairo, with Konzelmann in front of the camera and a stage behind him filled with upset chairs, soldiers, uncertainty, and turmoil. Only moments before, during a military parade, three soldiers jumped down from a convoy of trucks, ran up to the podium, and shot President Sadat. Eleven other visitors on the rostrum had been slain, and many more were injured. Konzelmann improvised a report on what had just happened; it was unclear whether the shooting had ended or Sadat was still alive; he had been apprehended by security troops. Calm, concentrated, and sweating, Konzelmann provided the clearest explanation of the Egyptian state's underlying inconsistencies that I have ever heard, as well as reporting on the origins and role of the Egyptian Muslim Brotherhood, the most likely group behind the assassination. So this was the man I had phoned a few years ago about the documentary series he was creating and met in Stuttgart's cafeteria. I had a film in mind that would be ideal for his series, and Konzelmann enthusiastically agreed during our chilly lunch. The downside for me was that his series did not include an anonymous off-air commentary; instead, each of the filmmakers had to appear as the narrators of their films and speak to the camera. So I'd have to appear. I opposed the concept for a long time, but it resulted in me never leaving my voice-over to someone else and always recording it myself. This was a step with far-reaching consequences that I did not anticipate. It led to me discovering my voice, or stage voice, if you will.

I had an immediate connection with Walter Steiner. At the customary Vierschanzentournee Tournee, or Four Hills Tournament, at the close of 1973 and the beginning of 1974, he was far down in the field due to an injury, a broken rib. When many questioned if I was backing a lame horse, I remained optimistic. I assured him at the ski jumping contest in Planica, Slovenia, that he would outperform the rest. Perhaps this gave him confidence, but it was more than that; physical intimacy was sometimes crucial in my work with actors or documentary subjects. Bruno S., the lead in two of my films, The Enigma of Kaspar Hauser and Stroszek, grew irritated at times by the horrors of the environment he had grown up in. I would grab his wrist, which calmed him down.

In Planica, Steiner was so amazing that he nearly died multiple times since the ramp was not designed for a flyer like him. To explain, when the skier jumps, he lands on a steep downward slope, and his kinetic energy is reduced. Even falls that appear to be dramatic are rarely severe. However, if one were to fall on the flat after an extremely long jump, which no one had anticipated, the deceleration would be rapid, just as a jump from a twentieth-story window onto a paved road is fatal. The huge ramp at Planica, like practically all other ramps in existence, has a sector-shaped radius that rapidly transitions from steep to flat. The important point in the race is when the radius begins, which is always marked by a red line in the snow. If a jumper flies past that point, the technical officials are required to immediately stop the competition and continue with a shorter descent so that the jumpers do not cross the red line. However, Steiner flew so far past the vital point that he broke the previous world record by roughly ten metres. There were no more measuring boards where he had landed. The compression was so severe that the force of his landing forced him to crash.

He received a concussion, and for an hour he had no idea where he was or what had occurred. However, during the competition's final two days, the Yugoslav judges four times permitted him to start from too far back and fly into the death zone. They wanted to see the new world record, regardless of the repercussions. The ski jumping event attracted 50,000 spectators. "They want to see me bleed; they want me smashed to little pieces," says Steiner. He won the tournament with the largest lead ever recorded. Steiner then demanded—now that he had the ability to do so—that the courses be rebuilt, emphasising the importance of a differently computed mathematical curve in the transition from slope to level. So far as I know, none of the great courses today have a sector-shaped level, but rather a curve generated from Fibonacci numbers—similar to a spiral curve found in fossilised ammonites. The curvature is much longer, making it impossible to fly straight down onto level ground.

Chapter 5: FABIUS MAXIMUS AND SIEGEL HANS

At the Cannes picture Festival in the mid-1970s, the Lebanese French producer Jean-Pierre Rassam, who had just finished La Grande Bouffe in a mad race against time, proposed that we make a picture together. At that point, he had already gone bankrupt several times; he used narcotics, and he died of an overdose not long after that. But he was a crazy, productive man, and I adored him. I never cashed the check. For years, I kept it pinned above my desk to look at; the check outlasted Rassam.

Many years later, when a big portion of Germany's political establishment had abandoned any hope of reunification, I had the idea of following the border around my home country. Willy Brandt issued an official announcement stating that "the book of German reunification" was now closed in his opinion. At the time, he was pursuing a "small steps" policy, which entailed integrating the socialist GDR with the West through tiny, realistic, largely economic initiatives. There was also rationality in improving the lives of GDR residents; for example, one of my best cameramen, Jörg Schmidt-Reitwein, was released from his East German prison. A few days after they began erecting the Wall in 1961, he was arrested entering the GDR using a valid second passport for his fiancée in order to get her out. In a show trial, he was accused of working for the CIA after it was discovered that he had previously worked as an assistant cameraman for Sender Freies Berlin, which was partially funded by Americans. What I found uncomfortable at the time was that many intellectuals, like novelist Günter Grass, were fiercely opposed to the idea of German reunification. That is why I despised him so much. I was not surprised that Grass confessed to being in the SS shortly before his death, but I did admire his fortitude in dealing with his past. I believed only poets could hold Germany together. I wanted to create a loop around Germany to hold everything together like a belt.

I started at the Ölberg Chapel outside Sachrang on the Austrian border and climbed the Spitzstein as Siegel Hans had done. From there, I would follow the border west until the end of my tour of the country, when I would circle around on the eastern side of the Geigelstein.

Chapter 6: ALONG THE BORDER

All that remains of my notes are a few excerpts from a reasonable copy that I made some time ago. The remainder of the original disappeared sometime along the line. I began my lengthy march on June 15, 1982; subsequently, the document includes no dates.

From the Ölberg Chapel beside the customs post, I travelled through the gorgeous, towering woodlands toward Sachrang, which was soon gone from view as I rose fast past Mitterleiten. Construction equipment was crushing gravel. Next to it stood a brick structure that would never be finished. At Mitterleiten, I was overtaken by a local riding a motorcycle; I knew who he was, but he didn't recognize me when I said hi. I ascended rapidly, but my heart felt heavy. At the place where builders' rubble was dumped into the woods; where trucks drive their loads of crushed roof tiles through the trees; where the storm wind tugs at the great sheets of plastic, but they are held down like dead bodies by stones; where timid ducks, who must have had some experiences in the ugly little gravel pool of the never-completed excavation, flew away from me; at that point, after long bumbling about in my past, I left my beloved Sachra.

I exited Mittenwald at a jog-trot. I have never seen such a degraded landscape. Level sanded footpaths as seen in city parks, confected nature trails, warning signs pointing out dangers, and the unavoidable postscript that the community has no responsibility for anything. The Watzmann Peak stood in pale dusk light, its rocks appearing to chill by the minute. The Watzmann is a persistent mountain. Silence descended on the forest. On a pond in the moor, two wild ducks floated like ancient dreams. Walking beside a huge deer fence, I came across an almost industrial deer site, complete with large hay cribs, salt licks, observation posts, and a somewhat rough cabin. Two young stags and a female were grazing in a meadow in front of the trees; they gazed around and sniffed appreciatively for a minute. Who was this, then? Even if I was a stranger to myself, they had no idea. Herzog, I presented myself and offered my services, after which they vanished into the woods in a few grand steps.

I could see icefields stretching as far ahead of me as the glaciers and glacial tips of the Svalbard archipelago. They got closer and transformed into reality. I slipped and tumbled under the rails of an iced balcony of a baroque palais, plunging into the vast depths of glacier tongues that abruptly broke off in front of me into the Elbe. I'm not sure if it was the Elbe or the Siberian Yenisei. With the sudden shock, I saw my fall as my death, but tumbling through the air, I still had the presence of mind to spread my arms like a parachutist following the others of his unit, so, by directing my fall some hundreds of yards further on, I avoided the sharp edge of the ice and fell instead into the icy waters of the Elbe, which unfortunately carried no water but...

The slope to the Bayer Alp is steep, with several wretched dwellings in a narrow depression. This marks the start of the forest trail to Wildbad Kreuth. After several hours of rain on my descent, it suddenly became pitch-black, as if a cataclysmic storm was on its approach. I sought refuge on a bench beneath the overhanging roof of an abandoned cottage, and it wasn't long before a severe storm swept up the narrow valley, throwing grey and white shreds of mist into the tossing trees. When it became worse, and I assumed the tempest was reaching its peak, something else happened that made everything else seem like a little prelude. Foaming white waterfalls cascaded from the sheer cliff face opposite, and everything was shrouded in white racing clouds that ripped and momentarily revealed the tops of trees before swooping away in panic flight down the slope. The view opened up like a curtain tearing itself apart, revealing frothy and furious white waterfalls and streams of water that had not existed only moments before. The storm struck like

God's wrath on an infidel. I had to wait a long time for the worst to pass, staring at the enormous rage and knowing that I was the only one who saw it. In my oddly melancholy state, the idea of heading down into the valley, away from my border and into human habitation seems unbearable, so I selected the path west, sharply up into the mountains, even though the rain hadn't stopped. I began the steep ascent alongside a rushing torrent. The walkway had turned into a waterfall, which became heavier as I climbed. Before long, I was encircled by clouds. The horizon over the Wildermann col suddenly burst open, illuminated by yellow-orange rainlight. Vales, peaks, and woods appeared curiously vulnerable deep into the mountains, as if holding out a huge promise to a thirsty people, while an uncertain white sheet of fog bubbled up from the depths behind me. Then, with perfect theatricality, the stage closed behind me. I spent the evening in the cabin chatting to Germany's multiple whitewater champion from the 1950s, who told me about his life as a postwar athlete. When he was training alone, he would frequently cry from hunger.

In Strasbourg, I sat on a bench; eventually, a courteous Algerian joined me. A little later, a second Algerian arrived with a white plastic bag; he shook hands with his companion and, of course, with me as well. I was shaken. I'd passed into France. Across the Rhine, Germany appeared like a figment of someone's mind. In Strasbourg Cathedral, bikers strolled silently along the nave, only their leathers creaking. They carried their helmets beneath their arms, just like mediaeval knights. At night, the cows who shared my field murmured in their sleep.

I awoke early, with a start. I couldn't feel anything; Germany was gone, everything was gone; it was as if I had suddenly lost something that had been given to me the night before—or as if someone who was keeping watch over an entire army suddenly turned out to be blindfolded, leaving the army vulnerable. Everything was gone, and I felt absolutely empty, devoid of pain, pleasure, or desire. There was nothing left. I was like a castle with no knights inside. The shock did me good. Purple images settled over me.

I never finished my walk around the country. After travelling over a thousand kilometres, I became ill and had to spend several days in the hospital. In retrospect, I realise I would never have been able to stroll around the GDR since the police would not allow you to wander along the Baltic shore. There were too many fugitives leaving for Sweden or Denmark in rowboats and inner tubes. The fall of the Berlin Wall, which I saw as a signal for reunification, has left an indelible mark on my memories. I was filming in Patagonia at the time for my film Scream of Stone. We were in a rural location far from civilization, but a climber heard about it on his shortwave radio a few days later and informed me while we were filming. I still feel a strong sense of joy. We wrapped up the shoot early, and I drank Chilean wine with the guys. Germany and Bavaria are nothing more than an apparent contradiction in my eyes. First, Germany was never forged in the fires of history, and second, Bavaria has never been affiliated with my family over generations. Despite the fact that my family has different European ancestors, I am a Bavarian by culture. My native tongue is Bavarian; the environment is familiar, and I know where I live.

In Sachrang and the surrounding mountains, I was constantly on foot, and often barefoot. That took on a new meaning after I converted to Catholicism and hiked with a group of religiously inclined friends on the border of then-Yugoslavia and Albania. I'll explain more about that later. However, walking became increasingly essential and obvious in relation to my grandfather Rudolf, my father's father; I felt as if I was going through his landscapes. I was closer to him than my biological father. I believe it was due to the fact that the turn-of-the-century generation had deeper historical roots than my parents' generation, who chose National Socialism over the continuum of

European culture. They fell into a misty Germano-mystical archaism and perished with it. Perhaps I am focusing too much on my own family here. Families are odd things, and mine is no different. In addition, I only knew my grandfather after he had gone insane.

Chapter 7: ELLA AND RUDOLF

Such wealth is virtually unthinkable to me, and the concept of a stork fishing for goldfish in my grandmother's fountain in the heart of today's urban Frankfurt is simply impossible. But when my grandmother Ella married my grandfather, she left everything behind to live and work with him on the impoverished island of Cos—a Turkish colony at the time, but now Greek. Her encounter with my grandfather had been long planned. Her father had nursed his father-in-law through his latter years following a series of strokes. To reward him for his devoted care, he was sent on a Mediterranean cruise, where destiny intervened. He accompanied his daughter, first down the Rhine to Antwerp, where they boarded their ship and sailed around the coasts of France and Spain to Genoa and Naples. Ella was seventeen, tall, shapely, and attractive. Toward the end of the voyage, during an excursion to Capri, she was approached by a fellow passenger, Bülow, a chemical professor at Tübingen.

Ella only learnt years later via the Bülows' letters with her parents that she and Rudolf were purposefully seated together at several dinner invitations that came after that. She later received these letters as a gift and extensively quoted from them in her memoirs. From today's perspective, the steps are outstanding in their seriousness and punctuality, while always respecting Ella's feelings and ideas. The chemistry professor von Bülow was persuaded that his friend Rudolf Herzog, a young classics professor with a deep mind and heart, deserved a woman as splendid and attractive as Ella. However, my grandfather was a timid, introverted man who was incredibly inventive and has extraordinary leadership abilities.

Rudolf despatched a letter announcing his visit that day, but it was yet to arrive. Ella and Rudolf confessed their love at a brief intimate time during a trip into the country, when Ella's brother (chaperoning them) could be enticed away, and their engagement was celebrated that same afternoon. The wedding wasn't scheduled for another year, but a scant two weeks later, Rudolf wrote that he needed to go to Cos for an archeological expedition and that they couldn't marry immediately because he wanted Ella to accompany him. So the wedding took place after a brief engagement, and Ella wrote lovely letters home from her honeymoon.

During the last eight years of his life, he developed a progressive dementia. It wasn't Alzheimer's, but rather a sort of calcification. He no longer recognized anybody. My younger sister, Sigrid, my father's daughter from his second marriage, frequently visited Grosshesselohe, where Rudolf had constructed a house, and whenever her mother, Doris, arrived to pick her up, my grandfather was always distraught. He would stand by the garden gate and ask visitors for assistance; his daughter had been kidnapped and stolen, and he characterised the three-year-old as an angel of beauty and charm, which was a fitting description of my sister, as we all saw her that way. Several times, the police were summoned, and my grandmother would photograph them; several times, my grandfather was able to escape the locked garden and wander around in the adjacent woods in Pullach, which happened to be where the German intelligence services were headquartered.

Later, in 1967, when I was twenty-five years old and filming my first film, Signs of Life, in the same citadel on Cos, I inserted some of these inscriptions into a shot, and one of my characters translated the writing on a piece of stone in a courtyard. My grandfather's journey from classical philology to archaeology began with a meticulous analysis of an ancient text. The book in question was the Mimiambs of Herondas, a little-known dramatist from the third century BCE. Only a few lines of the book had previously been known, but it was discovered nearly full in 1890 on a well-preserved papyrus scroll in an Egyptian tomb in the Fayoum Oasis. What stands out is how prudish academicians in the late nineteenth century did everything they could to avoid calling a spade a spade. The sixth mimiambus sticks out slightly, and in a manner, it determines the trajectory of my grandfather's life. It depicts two women visiting the sanctuary of Asclepius, the god of medicine.

Following my grandmother's death, the house in Grosshesselohe collapsed. The generation that came after her was a waste. Beginning with my father, Dietrich, it was a lost generation. Rudolf and Ella had one further child, my aunt. I have the utmost regard for her since she was kind and steadfast, and she frequently gave my mother money in times of extreme need. My father never fulfilled his commitments and married twice more. Women were there to raise his children—we called them his second and third litters—and provide for their families. His sister married an undesirable character a few years before I was born; there were reports that he was a commoner, a prole who had never read a book, which seemed refreshing to me, but this man perished on the Eastern Front, or he acquired an ailment and died there. My aunt had a daughter with him, and she bravely accepted her fate by becoming a schoolteacher. My cousin and I were close. We grew up together and saw each other on family birthdays. My aunt first moved into my grandparents' house and later took over, and there was a Pakistani tenant on the first floor. I think he came to Germany during the upheaval of Partition.

After I grew up, I lost contact with my female cousin. She married an American mathematician who had a series of nervous breakdowns before returning to the States. My aunt joined them over there. They had an organic farm with goats, and they sold their milk and cheese at farmers' markets. My cousin had two children—a boy and a girl. Their circumstances must have been dreadful, with everyone always at each other's throats. The children threatened to murder the entire family once, and as they were under the age of eleven, they might have done so without incurring legal consequences. However, I only know about that aspect of the tragedy from secondhand accounts.

Chapter 8: ELISABETH AND DIETRICH

I know very little about my parents' meeting. On the surface, everything appears simple: they met as students in Munich, where they both studied biology and my mother minored in athletics. They were both early and devoted Nazi Party members. My mother's family has a history of aspiring Croatian nationalism, and there are rumours that some of her Stipetić relatives were implicated in the killing of Serbian King Alexander I. In a moment of candour, my mother showed me a photograph of some Austro-Hungarian soldiers posing ostentatiously near rebels hanging from posts, but the nationality of the deceased was unknown. My mother had a loaded revolver and was an excellent shot, but I believe she only had it after the divorce, when my father requested parental rights over me and my brother. My mother was actively active for the early Nazis when a student in Vienna, and she sought safety in Germany prior to the Anschluss. I believe she had been arrested, but she refused to discuss anything. It was an embarrassment to her, a horrible misjudgment, and when she arrived in Germany, she swiftly abandoned National Socialism and the political arena because she saw that it could only lead to disaster. She fully realised this by the time I was born, precisely when the tide changed with defeats in Russia and North Africa.

My father's Nazism stems from his ardent membership in student brotherhoods, which have served as a driving force for the German Reich from the early nineteenth century. Because he had attended several universities, he belonged to four different corps, all of which were so-called duelling fraternities, which meant that their members fought ritualised duels in which they cut each other's faces with sharp foils or sabres, resulting in so-called duelling scars or honour scars that could be seen from a long distance. My father was proud of the scars on his face, and it was his deepest dream that I, too, would one day study and join such a fraternity—his firstborn son, my brother

Tilbert, quickly proved to be a dud in school and dropped out early. The scars gave my father a dashing appearance, and he was constantly tanned, resembling a pirate rather than a professor.

All I remember about my parents' early relationship is that they went canoeing and camping down the Danube. When my father received his call-up paperwork, they married fast and suddenly. I never saw a wedding photograph. After the war, my father spent an additional year in a French POW camp. One day, a strange man appeared in our kitchen; my memory recalls him wearing a cream suit, but this is most likely a creation. My younger sibling was born during the divorce. My younger brother was given a terribly Germanic first name, which my mother was loath to use after a while—if ever. Instead, mom called him Xaverl, but we, his older brothers, didn't believe that was appropriate, so we called him Lucki. That stuck, and my brother continues to use it as if it were his given name.

We brothers were delighted to have a new addition to the family, but my mother was unable to support us without an income because our father never paid his alimony. When she was at the hospital in Wels, Austria, with Lucki, she met a family who realised how desperate she was and offered to take Lucki with them. He was then a small cherub who immediately won everyone's hearts. So Lucki ended up spending some time with "Uncle Heribert"'s family in Wels. He only joined the rest of us in Sachrang when he was four years old, and Till and I were thrilled to have him among us. Lucki later played an important role in my career. He remained by my side since Aguirre, the Wrath of God in 1972. He has exceptional organisational skills, and it is because of him that I have been able to do so much. He has exceptional musical abilities but realised early on that he will never be a concert pianist.

Till and I were placed with my father in Wüstenrot for a short period after Lucki's birth because my mother was unable to feed us. She was preparing to go to Munich, but she didn't yet have a job or a place to live. Wüstenrot is a self-styled spa town near Heilbronn and Schwäbisch Hall. Later on, when Till and I were set to start high school, we remained with my father again. We finished our last few months of elementary school there, and to our astonishment, we were taunted about our Bavarian dialect. It was there that I learnt High German as a second language. My Bavarian was so strong that my father could occasionally have required an interpreter. We were both accepted into the humanistic Theodor-Heuss-Gymnasium in Heilbronn, and I am grateful to my father for insisting on Latin and Greek education in accordance with family tradition. Back in Wüstenrot, he enthusiastically served us fried eggs in the village restaurant, which I believe were the first fried eggs I'd ever had.

In Wüstenrot, we started playing soccer with local lads and invariably ended up with muddy clothes. My father believed the game was too ordinary and suggested we practise something more sophisticated, such as fencing or field hockey. We were tried out at a hockey club in Heilbronn, and during one of the first practice sessions, I was hit in the shin with a ball. You must be aware that the balls are actually boulders the size of your fist, rather than balls. It was quite uncomfortable, and I developed a bump on the bone. That was sufficient for me. To conceal our comeback to soccer, we wore our game shorts underneath our normal attire, which we removed after school for our kickabouts in the cabbage fields.

When we were commuting to school in Heilbronn, the one-hour bus ride seemed long. We rode in a crude trailer that transported impoverished industrial workers to factories in the valley because it was less expensive. The trailer featured a small pot bellied burner, and the workers either played cards or slept. There was just one small window, and the air was dense with cigarette smoke. My father quickly got us a place to stay with a family in Heilbronn, but all I remember are the children. The oldest brother was named Klett, but I'm not sure if it was his first or last name. He had a lot of criminal energy and encouraged us to start shoplifting in department stores. It wasn't the kind of frivolous stealing that many kids engage in, but rather a deliberate act. Klett, who was only a year older than us, intended to get into carjacking, but by the time it happened, if it happened at all, we had left Heilbronn. I recall how, under his direction, we lifted a round manhole cover and covered it with old cement bags.

During this period, my mother sought to get us started in the city. There was no future for us in Sachrang; the only opportunities were as a woodcutter or cowherd. We had never been fully integrated into the hamlet; we were not outsiders, but they did treat us as newcomers. It seemed as if the other fleeing youngsters and the kids from the nearby farms were lured into our circle. Shortly after the war ended, the Marshall Plan brought us the first CARE packages, which helped us get through the worst. I will be forever grateful to America for them. The containers included corn flour, which we were unfamiliar with and found strange. My mother persuaded us to try it by explaining that the flour was yellow because it included egg yolks, which made it particularly nutritious. We continued to eat it happily after that. One of the first packets included a book written like a giant schoolbook: Winnie-the-Pooh. I admire the knowledge and compassion required to include such a statement. Probably no one knows who came up with such a concept, but I admire the person or people who did.

How we adored our modest abode. Today, it has been badly refurbished, with the entire back half, which used to be an airy barn, converted into apartments. But back then, there were inexplicable creakings and hauntings. Once, I ran into God there. I was around four years old, and my brother Till and I were bragging about how on Saint Nicholas Day, on the dark landing, we would set up a tripwire for Krampus, a kind of rustic devil in fur and horns that terrorised disobedient children with a heavy chain. We were ecstatic about the concept; we weren't scared at all; we outdid each other in our fearlessness. We also imagined that Saint Nick would stumble into our kitchen and land flat on his belly, causing all of the presents to fall out of his sack and freeing us from his admonitions. But as Saint Nicholas Day came, our courage appeared to dissipate. We never put up the tripwire. When I heard Krampus stamp his hooves on the landing and rattle his chain, I hid behind the sofa. The next thing I felt was Krampus grab me by the seat of my pants and drag me out. I stood there, and I believe I wet myself. But then I saw God, and He smiled at me. He leaned against the doorjamb, wearing washed brown overalls with thick oil stains, and I knew I'd been spared. It was God. Much later, I learned that the man came from the small electrical shack in the ravine by the waterfall and followed Nicholas inside the house. There was a little generator in the forest that ran on water from the stream and that this man occasionally checked to lubricate. Electricity was seldom guaranteed in the early postwar years. Often, there was only candlelight in the kitchen.

The relocation to the city was unavoidable. We knew little about the world outside the valley. Aschau, twelve kilometres away, represented the end of the known world. Rosenheim appeared as a faint glimmer in the sky. On rare occasions, cars appeared from there, and when we noticed one, we dashed to look at it. Once, on a hairpin turn, one lost control and plunged into the creek directly under Sturm Ötz. We'd often assemble there in the hopes of witnessing another tragedy. We once observed Siegel Hans riding his motorcycle around the corner laying over and accelerating away. Since then, I've been captivated by cars—at least when I watch them.

Chapter 9: MUNICH

Before moving there, we had only gone to Munich once. There were still large piles of rubble around the central station, and my brother and I greeted everyone who passed us on the street, hundreds of them, like we had done on Sachrang's village street. We also pulled down the fronts of our lederhosen and peed in the street. For the first time in her life, my mother disowned us. Then, a few years later, while we were visiting our father in Wüstenrot, mom looked for housing for us and paid her way with intermittent employment as a cleaning woman and a sort of peddler with a female acquaintance. Nylon stockings were sold to extras at the newly reopened film studios on the outskirts of town at Geiselgasteig. My mother did it all without complaint, driven by pragmatism and willpower. She worked as a housekeeper for an American occupying commander for a time, although she rarely mentioned it after that. She cleaned the flat, did the laundry, and cooked; but the man's wife made her life miserable.

All we remember is how things felt, but combat is always horrific, and it tends to get worse as technology advances. Two things stayed with me as reminders of that time. When there was food on the table, I had to eat quickly or my brothers would eat it all. Even today, I rush my food, despite telling myself to chew each piece and eat mindfully. The second issue is that I have difficulties throwing away food, particularly bread. My refrigerator is always well-maintained. It's mind-boggling to me that in the developed world, 40% of all food is wasted; the proportion in the United States appears to be considerably higher. I'm rarely surrounded by people who have had similar childhood experiences, so I watch silently while large quantities are served in restaurants, half of which end up in waste. The consumerist mania has spread throughout the industrialised globe, causing immense damage to our planet's health. Obesity, which affects so many people, is just one visible aspect of consumerism. Even though I periodically find rotting lettuce in my fridge, I rarely throw anything away.

The pension on Elisabethstrasse was a rambling old-fashioned property with five or six rooms rented out. Clara Rieth, the owner, grew up in Munich's creative Schwabing milieu in the 1920s, when it was the city's bohemian district. It's been a long time since there were artists living there, just as Paris' Montmartre quarter ultimately froze into its own monument while preserving some of the late nineteenth century for tourists. Then, in the 1960s and 1970s, when the New German Cinema emerged, practically all of the directors lived in Schwabing, while Munich was Germany's cultural capital. When Berlin replaced Bonn as Germany's capital, practically everyone departed to go there. Clara was particularly interested in theatre and art, and she went around looking very striking, with her hair painted a vibrant orange, much like the punks would do decades later. In the vast corridor of her apartment, one section was separated by a heavy curtain, behind which lived my mother's acquaintance who sold stockings with her.

Till and I were accepted into the humanistic Maximilian Gymnasium in Munich. The school had a remarkable reputation. In addition to giving eight years of Latin and six years of Greek, it established high standards in arithmetic, science, literature, and art. Max Planck and Werner Heisenberg, two of the twentieth century's greatest theoretical physicists, studied here. It's difficult to describe the significance of dead languages to people today. Latin is useful in a pinch, but only for lawyers, theologians, and historians. In a purely practical sense, these languages are pointless. However, their research provided us with a more in-depth understanding of the beginnings of Western culture, literature, philosophy, and the most fundamental currents of our view of the world we live in. I must admit that I always felt like a stranger there, but only to the other students, who were all from prosperous middle-class homes.

By the second year of his studies at the Maximilian Gymnasium, it was evident that he lacked patience and knowledge of Latin. He failed the course and had to repeat the year. From then on, I had a brother who was a year older than me and a year behind me in school. He received the "lap of honour" but then failed the next class, putting him two years behind me. At fourteen, he impulsively fled the unwanted and inadequate school. He was apprenticed at a lumber company, and his career took off. At the age of 21, he was the head of acquisitions and sales, driving a business Mercedes, and a few years later, he co founded a trading company in partnership with a largely state-owned Yugoslav company with ties to China. This company flourished swiftly, establishing furniture plants in Manchuria and Sichuan, where Till's firm exported all of its machinery. Till was in China for many weeks at the time with a Yugoslav group. Later, a similarly structured Yugoslav corporation in the leather and footwear industry purchased Till's company, resulting in the production of approximately five million pairs of high-quality shoes in Italy, Yugoslavia, and Russian markets.

In its peak years, his company's revenue exceeded 100 million marks, with very profitable partnerships centred on Yugoslavia. Till was burned out at the age of 51, having worked hard for 36 years. He later informed me, rather bluntly, that if he had stayed, he would have died within a year due to managerial stress. He sold his shares, and his high pay as manager, along with annual bonuses, ensured he would never have to work again. He cruised the Mediterranean and Caribbean on his yacht. Then he built himself a lavish villa on the Costa Blanca. He now shuttles between Munich and Spain. He has been happily married for 47 years and has two great boys.

While Till began his business career, my mother took a full-time job in a well-established antique shop specialising in art and first editions, where the exceedingly wealthy proprietors paid her a scandalously low pay. Meanwhile, they made sure their consumers knew she was academically trained and had a doctorate. Her salary would not have supported a family of four. My brother quickly became the primary income, and if it hadn't been for him, I would have struggled to stay in school, despite the fact that I was also working. In my free time, I worked as a labourer, stacking planks. It was purely physical effort.

In the top levels of the gymnasium, I alternated between two parallel classes, one for Catholics and one for Lutherans. This was due in part to my conversion to Catholicism, but also because I did not always follow the school calendar. I hitchhiked to northern Germany with my brother the same year he started working. Because the school had enrolled another student in my place the second time and the class was now full, I was assigned to a parallel class of Protestants. Today, I am pleased because I made two friends who are essential to me. One was Rolf Pohle, a musician who played the violin. He suffered from awful acne, not just on the surface, but deep within his psyche. In soccer games, he was a tenacious defender, a terrier; you dribbled around him just to find him facing you again two paces later. Rolf went on to study law, shifted his ideology to the left, became the head of AStA at Munich University in 1967, and in 1968, he organised rallies in Munich despite police restrictions during the so-called Easter Riots. That resulted in a court appearance, and shortly before his final examinations, he was barred from studying law. This radicalised him even further. He became involved with the Baader-Meinhof Group and the RAF, and went underground. Because he held a legitimate firearms licence, he became a supplier of pistols for violent purposes. He vanished from my consciousness entirely until he caused a car accident on a winter road near Augsburg. He ran on foot over a frozen field, vanished, and was eventually apprehended at the end of 1971.

His sentence was eventually enhanced. In 1975, he was one among six convicts scheduled to be traded for Berlin politician Peter Lorenz. Lorenz was kidnapped by the 2 June Movement, which supported the

RAF. The prisoner exchange took place, and Rolf and the other released inmates were taken to Aden, the communist People's Democratic Republic of South Yemen. However, when the state released them and handed them money, Rolf most likely wanted a larger payment than what was offered—at least that is what was later said. Because this was seen as extortion, he ended up serving a couple more years in prison when he was recaptured in Greece and extradited to Germany. I never saw him again. He left Germany, married his Greek defender, and took up residency in Greece. I heard he was seriously unwell. He died in Athens in 2004; the declared cause was cancer, but unofficially it was AIDS.

He was a gift to me. Finally, someone with the fire inside them that I really missed. The University of Munich recognized his outstanding talent and permitted him to begin studies while still in high school. At the time of his school final exams, he had already completed six semesters of German at the university. He and I approached things very differently; he laid out his arguments in detail and demonstrated the entire scintillating complexity of a thought, which led him to continue fiddling with his dissertation and doctorate, whereas I concentrated on the bold outlines and went for the heart of a problem. However, he was an enthusiast, and I lit his flame. It was via him that I discovered the first mention of Lope de Aguirre for my film Aguirre, the Wrath of God. I visited him once, and he barely acknowledged me before returning to his phone. He had a crush on someone. I realised he didn't have time for me, so I went through the endless rows of his books. I took one down at random since it appeared to stick out. It was a book about discoverers aimed at twelve-year-olds. Vasco da Gama and Columbus appeared in it, but it was a single little paragraph of around ten lines that piqued my interest.

I had never been particularly interested in literature or history in school, but it was probably just part of my sour attitude toward the place. I was an autodidact by nature, but as soon as gymnasium ended, I applied to university to study history and literature. But my studies were a fake; I knew this from the start because I was already working on my first films and needed money to support them. Even physically, I was rarely present; there were semesters when I only turned up once or twice.

Chapter 10: SECOND MEETING WITH GOD

Despite my new acquaintances from the other class, the Catholic stream left an imprint on my life that lasted long after I graduated. My brothers and I had grown up without religion, as heathens. I never mentioned it until one day at Sachrang, when the local priest yelled at us for being godless and slapped my older brother in the face. We could have been six or seven at the time. Our parents were both atheists, with my father being quite ardent. Later, when I was thirteen, I began to have a sense of emptiness. I was restless because I craved transcendence and sublimity. People close to me, such as my brother Till, never caught on. He assumed I had fallen for our current religious studies instructor, a Catholic priest. We referred to him as der Läben because of his sheepish bleat when he talked about "das äwige Läben" (for das ewige Leben, eternal life), but that would be an oversimplification. Friends assumed that my conversion to Catholicism was a form of protest against my father, but this was a naive and dumb notion because, after all, my mother was also an atheist.

Arianism was branded a heresy by the Council of Nicaea in AD 325, yet I would have preferred to side with the heretics. My sympathies were with Pelagius, a thinker who was declared a heretic by the Council of Ephesus in AD 431. He is considered the father of free will in Catholic theology during the end of the fourth and early fifth centuries. His reasoning was that man is endowed with the moral ability to avoid sin, and thus possesses free will. Saint Augustine prevailed in his belief that original sin is inherent in humanity and that there could be no existence without sin if it were not for God's grace. Non posse non peccare, it is impossible for me not to sin, was his famous saying. Personally, I would consider Augustine, the church father, to be a heretic before Pelagius. And I'd like to comment about the Bavarian Pope Benedict XVI, who led the Roman Catholic Church from 2005 to 2013. I loved him because he was intellectually rigorous. His public appearances as pope were generally well-received, but his public relations management was disastrous.

To begin, there was a brief phase of devoutness. It's difficult for me to understand right now; it puzzles me. I was temporarily an altar boy, but my brother Till made fun of me, and I realised I'd soon wind myself in some amen corner. I desired a more extreme kind of Christianity, so I joined a group my age known as the Association of Saints. We imagined an idealised vision of early Christianity that very definitely never existed. Father Leppich, a Jesuit, was our living idol, and his street assemblies drew throngs across Germany. Leppich's extremism made him alluring to youths. On closer examination, his demagogy bothered me. It quickly became repulsive, and my time as a radical had come to an end. The saints' association was inspired by the German Wandervogel movement of the early twentieth century, and we travelled in their spirit on multiple occasions, the first of which was to Lake Ohrid, which borders Yugoslavia, Greece, and Albania. We also hiked near the Albanian border. Albania continues to interest me. Following the end of World War II, Enver Hoxha envisioned it as a stronghold of Chinese Communism, keeping it separate from the Soviet Union.

Many of my films include a distant echo of deity or transcendence. Even some of the titles appear to indicate this: Every Man for Himself and God Against All; Aguirre, the Wrath of God; The Lord and the Laden; Huie's Sermon; God's Angry Man; and Bells from the Deep, a film on faith and superstition in Russia. In 2017, I had a public talk with curator Paul Holdengräber, whose keen understanding of cultural links I admire.

Chapter 11: CAVES

There was an earlier version of this desire for transcendence. I refer to it as the time of my spiritual awakening, and I have no reservations about using such a lofty term for it. It was the first time I began to think and feel for myself outside of school or upbringing. I was twelve or thirteen, and we had just arrived in Munich. I walked past a bookstore without glancing at the display, yet something there prompted me to stop. I walked back to see. What I had noticed out of the corner of my eye was an image of a horse on a book jacket, but it was unlike any other picture I had ever seen. It was a book about cave paintings, and the image was one of the famous wall paintings from Lascaux. I glanced closer and realised from the book's subtitle that it contains Upper Paleolithic artwork created approximately 17,000 years ago. It made my spine tingle. I had to acquire the book, even though it was extremely expensive. I began earning money as a ball boy at certain tennis courts. Every week, I snuck past the bookstore to see if the book was still there. I was terrified that someone would have spotted it and taken it. I was in a state of panic. I assumed the book only existed in one copy. After two months, I had saved enough money, and the book was still there. I've never forgotten the shiver I felt when I opened it, turned the pages, and saw the images. Many decades later, I had the opportunity to shoot a film on the Chauvet Cave. Before entering politics, he was an actor, author, and director who had watched my films as a critic. He was about to say his well-planned "but unfortunately" when I interrupted him. I just stated that I knew I had the chops, as did numerous other filmmakers, but I also had a fire within me since I was thirteen years old. I told him about my awakening. The minister then leaned across the table to shake my hand.

The filming limits were harsh. Because the hundred thousand annual tourists to Lascaux had defiled the cave with their exhalations, they wanted to do it right in Chauvet. We were allowed to take only what we could carry. There were only four people, including myself, allowed to work in the cave at any given time, for a maximum of four hours per day. The filming was scheduled to last less than a week. One could only move on a two-foot-wide metal grid, and our lights were not to emit any heat—all completely fair limitations. There was no way to get help from outside because it would have required opening and closing a steel door. As a result, we created a very compact 3-D camera made up of two cameras connected in parallel that were a little bigger than matchboxes. I was accompanied by cameraman Peter Zeitlinger, his assistant Erik Söllner, both Austrians who were resolute, powerful, and experienced, as well as Estonian digital genius Kaspar Kallas. Kaspar had directed his own films, invented crucial software for James Cameron's Avatar, and was an accomplished cameraman.

Then, deep inside the Chauvet Cave, there is a pendulous fragment of rock that resembles a pine cone. The only depiction of a human in the cave is the bottom half of a naked woman embracing a bison's hooves. Thirty thousand years later, Picasso created his Femme et Minotaur lithograph series, which appears to have been influenced by the Chauvet cave. But Picasso, of whom I have no high regard, had died long before the cave was discovered. However, I wonder if there is anything like buried memories within families. Or, to put it another way, do we have pictures that lie dormant within us until they are awakened by a sudden shock? I believe so, and all of my works have explored such ideas, whether it was the ten thousand windmills of Crete in my first feature film, Signs of Life, or the steamship carried over a mountain, the key metaphor of my film Fitzcarraldo. I know that's a fantastic metaphor, but I don't know what it means.

Chapter 12: THE VALLEY OF THE TEN THOUSAND WINDMILLS

I stumbled upon Crete's windmills. It occurred during one of my early ventures; I am no longer clear of the timing. I had previously visited Crete with friends from the "group of saints," but we were largely in the middle and west of the island, in Rethymnon and Chania, as well as Hora Sfakion in the south. And I returned to the route of my grandfather Rudolf shortly after finishing school. I had Cretan friends in Munich with whom I had begun to speak Greek. Then, in the summer, I joined a convoy of used trucks from Munich, each with a car or two put on board.

I recently discovered an old photo of me with a shotgun in hand. A partridge dangles from my belt, and I'm wearing a tied handkerchief to protect my head from the sun. I'm standing there in profile, possibly to show off my partridge. I had developed into a fit-looking young man, but when I arrived in Africa, I was unwell and terribly shrunken. Another photo shows me in Crete riding on a donkey that I had hired for a few weeks. I called him Gaston; I can't remember why, but it seemed significant to me at the time. I went almost the entire length of the oblong island, not along the coast but across the highlands in the interior, following the donkey that carried water and food. I was fully alone, and I enjoyed the fact that I was now an independent adult. When Gaston came to a halt, I paused as well, and when, after some consideration, he chose to continue, so did I. In the far east of the island, I came to a ridge where the rock abruptly tumbled away. Perfectly unprepared from one minute to the next, I saw below me a large valley full of thousands of windmills all in motion, their white canvas sails moving like a meadow full of thousands of mad spinning flowers, a field of demented daisies.

Three years later, I completed the screenplay for Signs of Life. The protagonist, a World War II German soldier with a head wound, is sent alongside a few buddies to protect a fort where, bored, they let off fireworks made from explosives. On a reconnaissance excursion in the mountains, the patrol arrives at the location where I first noticed the windmills. When he sees them, the soldier loses control of his mind and begins shooting recklessly. From the fort, he strikes the harbour and town with horizontally aimed pyrotechnics, declares war on both friends and foes, and eventually shoots at the rising sun. Finally, he is overpowered by his own men.

There are some recurring themes in my films that are virtually always based on personal experience. I worked as a spot welder on the nightshift, which wasn't awful because night work was paid extra, but I also had to go to school during the day, which I barely registered for due to exhaustion. We were also constantly exposed to flying particles of burning metal, which posed a risk. I always worked in a leather apron, but late at night, I became less cautious, and some of the incandescent fragments would bounce off the apron and occasionally settle inside my shoes at over a thousand degrees centigrade. I'd hit the roof in agony, but by the time I took off my shoes, I had burns. The insides of my feet were always blistered.

Three years later, I completed the screenplay for Signs of Life. The protagonist, a World War II German soldier with a head wound, is sent alongside a few buddies to protect a fort where, bored, they let off fireworks made from explosives. On a reconnaissance excursion in the mountains, the patrol arrives at the location where I first noticed the windmills. When he sees them, the soldier loses control of his mind and begins shooting recklessly. From the fort, he strikes the harbour and town with horizontally aimed pyrotechnics, declares war on both friends and foes, and eventually shoots at the rising sun. Finally, he is overpowered by his own men.

There are some recurring themes in my films that are virtually always based on personal experience. I worked as a spot welder on the nightshift, which wasn't awful because night work was paid extra, but I also had to go to school during the day, which I barely registered for due to exhaustion. We were also constantly exposed to flying particles of burning metal, which posed a risk. I always worked in a leather apron, but late at night, I became less cautious, and some of the incandescent fragments would bounce off the apron and occasionally settle inside my shoes at over a thousand degrees centigrade. I'd hit the roof in agony, but by the time I took off my shoes, I had burns. The insides of my feet were always blistered.

Chapter 13: CONGO

Another factor that influenced my decision to leave school was time. From Crete, I boarded a ferry to Alexandria. I chose the cheapest class available and slept on deck to make my money go further. As soon as I set foot on the African continent in Alexandria, I was duped. A uniformed official demanded a ten-dollar landing charge and handed me a receipt. Only after I had paid did I realise that no one else had been asked to pay this price. The Egyptians, of course, didn't, and a few Greeks scoffed at the ruse. From then on, I was more cautious.

In 1992, while I was the director of the Viennale film festival in Vienna, I invited Ryszard Kapuściński, a Polish writer and philosopher. He knew more about Africa than anyone I knew, and a year before me, a young guy from Juba had reached eastern Congo. He was arrested forty times in a year and a half, four of which resulted in death sentences. I asked him how his worst day had been. The worst day lasted a week, during which he was in a pit under sentence of death while inebriated troops threw deadly snakes at him.

I wanted to make a science fiction film with him, but I wanted it to be unique. Science fiction depicts technological advancements in a futuristic world, or aliens visit us to destroy us with superior technology and futuristic weapons, but I was fascinated—as was he—by the idea that the future might be one in which we had lost all of our technological prowess, just as the fall of the Roman Empire resulted in the loss of almost every innovation in technology, medicine, science, mathematics, and literature. For the better part of the following thousand years, only fragments of ancient wisdom remained, concealed in monasteries or preserved in translations into Arabic. The worst loss of all was the fire that destroyed Alexandria's library, which housed the whole wealth of ancient knowledge, literature, and philosophy.

Chapter 14: DR. FU MANCHU

I was convinced that I would not make it to my eighteenth birthday. Once I had passed it, it seemed unlikely that I would ever be older than twenty-five. As a result, I began making films, expecting them to be all that remained of me. Why not try to find forms that never existed? Last Words, a 1967 modern Greek short with infinite, compulsive repetitions; Fata Morgana, a 1970 film in which I recorded mirages in the Sahara; and Even Dwarfs Started Small, another 1970 picture in which all of the characters are small people.

I wasn't impressed by the first two films I saw, which were projected onto a bedsheet in the Sachrang schoolhouse. The first was about Inuits building an igloo, and I could tell right away that they had no idea how to operate with ice and packed snow. Perhaps they had actors portraying Inuits. The second was far more intriguing; it depicted Pygmies in Cameroon, I believe, constructing a hanging bridge from lianas across a forest river. Their construction was wonderfully braided, a work of art in effect. Later, unlike my brothers and friends, I didn't find films very impressive when I first started going to the movies in Munich. When I realised what life had in store for me shortly after turning fourteen, when I converted to Catholicism and began travelling on foot, I knew I had to make films.

My mother was always sceptical of my filmmaking ambitions. In her opinion, I was too shy and introverted. But there was something in me that Catholics term "certainty of salvation." She wrote to me while I was on the road, suggesting that I establish a solid foundation for my wild dreams and apprentice myself to a photographer; that way, I could get a job in a film studio and possibly become someone's assistant director. There was no film school at the time, so I'm sure she would have advised it. She knew a props man from her time in Geiselgasteig in the Bavarian film studios, and she persuaded him to let me spend the day in the studio to observe what the job entailed.

A few years later, when I was considering shooting short films, I wondered if I should create my own production company. For me, the answer seemed obvious. I would never find a producer for my type of picture, so I'd have to do everything myself. That's why I began earning money while still in school. There was one incident that I recall vividly: a film producer responded positively to an outline I gave, but I realised I couldn't reveal myself. I was fifteen at the time, but I was still physically a child, with a growth spurt and puberty arriving late. The negotiations began with an exchange of letters, followed by a phone conversation. I believe it was my first phone call ever; I was desperate not to be spotted. Today, it's difficult to imagine.

There appeared to be no choice to begin my own business. My mother expressed alarm about the prospect. Finally, she suggested that I consult the spouse of one of her acquaintances in Aschau and seek his advice. This man was a remarkable financial supervisor in the early years of the Federal Republic. His name was Professor Wagner, and he had previously held government positions. As far as I recall, he was now a major player in the Montanunion, which finally became the EU. He was undeniably a man of immense personal influence and financial power. Wagner listened briefly to what I said before lecturing me in his booming voice about the complexities of the film industry. I was clearly not in my right mind; I needed to go away and study economics and possibly law, and then learn something about finance, ideally by working for a large corporation.

There was a film and television institute where I could meet people my age who shared my outlook. We were committed to supporting one another's endeavours. The institute predated the Munich Film Academy, and I was drawn to it since it housed cameras, sound equipment, and cutting tables. If you were selected, you were given the equipment for free, but all of my applications were rejected, and I was forced to watch as blatantly untalented people received cameras. With the exception of Uwe Brandner, who began as a musician, went on to make a few films, and eventually became a writer, none of the individuals I knew there ever achieved success. I learnt the fundamentals of cinema in about a week by reading the thirty or forty chapters on radio, film, and television in an encyclopaedia. I still believe that's all there is to know. Studying literature does not make you a poet, nor does typing. I understood the operation of a camera, how the film travelled, and what an optical soundtrack was.

Around that time, my brother Lucki finished school and, like my older brother, began working for a timber company. He, too, rose quickly, although he relocated to Essen before moving to Northern Germany. He had never joined Till and me in our soccer games or other activities because he was five years younger. During his time in Munich, he performed in a well-known boys' chorus and briefly considered a career in music. At the age of nineteen, he was a little concerned since he could see his entire professional career ahead of him, all the way to retirement. So he decided to quit and travel the world instead. He owned a Volkswagen Beetle and intended to drive to Turkey. I encouraged him to be more ambitious and travel farther afield, and he ended up driving from Anatolia to Afghanistan, then across the Khyber Pass to Pakistan and India, then to Nepal, and eventually to Indonesia, where he got a job teaching English at a private school. This, to him, was an unforgettable period of independence and adventure. Despite the fact that we were physically separated for much of our lives, he eventually joined me when I was busy preparing for Aguirre, the Wrath of God in Peru. From Indonesia, he travelled through Mexico to Lima. He played a vital role in my work and enterprise, giving organisation, collaboration, and efforts. Without his intervention, I would probably never have directed an opera, and without his foresight, there would be no charity organisation that now oversees all of my films and literary works. He and I complemented each other perfectly. I believe he was an excellent contrast to me over the years, behaving strategically while I was putting out flames. I was on the front lines, examining all of the forward outposts; he was the calm presence, deftly plucking strings in the background. For anyone who was broken, despondent, or desperate, he was always the final resort.

Chapter 15: JOHN OKELLO

Reading Lucki's old letters, I discovered interesting details of his travels to South India, Goa, Kathmandu, and Jakarta. By chance, there were also some letters from Field Marshal John Okello, who impacted the portrayal of my Aguirre in Aguirre, the Wrath of God. Okello, an orphan, arrived from northern Uganda. He grew up impoverished, supported himself through labour, and only attended school for a few years. He wandered around Uganda and Kenya before becoming an apprentice carpenter. In Uganda, he served a two-year prison sentence for an undefined sexual conduct, which he consistently disputed. Later, he worked as a mason, a trader, and a travelling preacher. He travelled to Zanzibar, where he was politicised at an early age. He has remarkable oratorical skills and was an excellent farmworker organiser. Zanzibar was traditionally the largest Arab-run slave-trading station in East Africa. In the twentieth century, the Arabs remained the dominant power, while being only a small fraction of the African people. Okello led an uprising against the Arabs that began without guns, uniforms, training, or money.

At a news conference two days following his insurrection, Okello explained that he had served as a brigadier general in Kenya's Mau Mau independence movement for the previous ten years and worked as a dream interpreter. He transcribed and interpreted the dreams of the entire rebel hierarchy, including its commander, Jomo Kenyatta. This strikes me as improbable, given Okello would have been barely seventeen, and the Kikuyu-dominated Mau Mau would scarcely have looked to an outsider from the Ugandan Acholi tribe, who had only recently begun to learn Swahili, Kenya's major language. Following the success of his revolution in Zanzibar, Okello recalled former Prime Minister Karume from exile on the mainland and reinstated him in power, but Zanzibar and Tanganyika on the mainland were plotting a union of their governments, which would be called

Tanzania.

Two years ago, I made a video in Kenya, Tanzania, and Uganda for an international medical organisation that was somewhat similar to Médecins Sans Frontières; the film was titled The Flying Doctors of East Africa. The cameraman was Thomas Mauch, who had worked on my picture Signs of Life, which was shot on Cos, and with whom I went on to produce a number of films, including Aguirre and Fitzcarraldo. Mauch was a formative figure for me; he was prepared for everything, confident in his manner, and had an incredible aesthetic sense while remaining strong and self-assured about the substance and dynamics of a scene. Cameramen are my eyes. I've worked with the best—Thomas Mauch, Jörg Schmidt-Reitwein, and later Peter Zeitlinger, with whom I created my last twenty-eight films. Cinematographers always set the tone for a film crew. After we finished our 1969 film about the flying physicians, Thomas Mauch and I flew to Uganda to hunt for John Okello. We drove across Kenya to Uganda because I had heard stories that Okello was in northern Uganda, where he was from. We arrived in the small town of Lira, where we looked about and eventually found some of his family, who appeared hesitant to give us information. He was presumably assassinated by Idi Amin in 1971, and the man I was thinking of was a Spanish conquistador. However, Aguirre's crazy speeches bear similarities to Okello. The video also has a Black slave that the conquerors take with them. I gave him the name Okello.

Chapter 16: PERU

Lucki travelled to Lima from another world. The startlingly wealthy daughter of one of Indonesia's top officials had wanted to marry him, and he was relieved to have avoided that fate. However, there were no telephone communications. When he arrived, we had no idea. There was no one to meet him at the airport, and no one staffed our small downtown office. I'd just set off for the jungle on the opposite side of the Andes. However, the flight was cancelled due to severe rains. I returned to the city in the middle of the night and ran across my brother, who I hadn't seen in years. The excitement of the meeting is still evident for me today. Lucki immediately seized the initiative, brought order to everything, and established a functional bookkeeping system, which was not an easy task because certain agreements had been made with people who could not read or write, and numerous documents had been washed away in tropical rain. He attempted to oversee the finance, but it was nearly impossible because there was practically none. The film's total budget was around $380,000, which was a joke for a major picture set in a jungle in the middle of the sixteenth century, complete with costumes, weapons, llamas, and rafts, not to mention about 400 Quechua-speaking highland Indigenous extras.

Lucki stated that he required $50,000 in Peruvian soles straight away. In exchange, he would have that amount wired from Germany to the United States, plus an additional 10% as a prize for such faith; the money would arrive within forty-eight hours. People in Lima had read about my idea in the newspapers, but who would sign up for it in the middle of the night in response to a knock on the door? Lucki, on the other hand, possessed a natural ability to build trust, which he understood better than to misuse. Joe Koechlin von Stein, a fairly young entrepreneur, accepted his offer. He needed money since he was organising a rock performance with Carlos Santana. With no guarantee other than a handshake, he handed Lucki the soles the next day, and the project was temporarily salvaged. Meanwhile, my brother Till sent $50,000 from his own cash to Joe's account in Miami. He, too, saved Aguirre, the Wrath of God, although secretly believing he would never see his money again. After a long wait, he did. I remain friends with Joe Koechlin to this day. He created the first eco-hotels in the Peruvian jungle, long before anyone had heard of the term "ecology."

Aguirre, the Wrath of God is about a group of Spanish conquistadors in the Amazonian lowlands looking for the fabled golden city of El Dorado. Lope de Aguirre organises a rebellion, and in his insane desire for power and fortune, the expedition devolves into a disastrous cycle of deception and self-destruction. In the end, Aguirre is left as the sole survivor on a raft covered in hundreds of little monkeys, drifting toward nowhere. From start to finish, the filming was fraught with uncertainty and risk. We were all living, drifting, and shambling around on our rafts—the actors, the tiny technical crew of eight—and the actual raft we were shooting was always one or two bends in the river ahead of us. We rarely knew what awaited us around the next corner. While we were filming, our whole stock of negatives vanished without trace. We had arranged with a shipping company in Lima to transfer the exposed photographs to Mexico City, where they would be developed, but the Mexicans swore blind that nothing ever arrived. We only had negatives. Without them, all would be lost. We had two suspicions: perhaps the Mexican print lab had made a terrible error and destroyed the negatives with the improper chemicals, so they were now pretending they never received them in the first place.

I recall there being times when there was nothing to eat, so one night, I and a few others set out in dugout boats to an Indigenous settlement in search of food. Once, I traded my nice shoes for a bathtub full of fish, and another time I left my wristwatch as payment. I recall one night paddling out and meeting at a curve in the river. Neither of the three of us had found anything. We tied our canoes together at four a.m. and drifted downstream while crying.

My brothers, especially Lucki, taught me not just how to inspire confidence, but also how to reward it unreservedly. For example, in 2015, we were in North Korea filming my film Into the Inferno, which I filmed with volcanologist Clive Oppenheimer and toured the world. After a year of negotiations, Clive was able to gain authorization to film there, which was extraordinary in and of itself. There were obviously limitations to what we could photograph, and we were constantly monitored by security personnel. However, we were allowed to film on the crater rim of Paektu Mountain. Conditions were much tougher than usual because the volcano was so close to the Chinese border. Many North Koreans attempted to flee across the border here, and there were numerous barricades guarded by soldiers. I noted that all of their automatic rifles were equipped with bayonets—not decorative bayonets like those seen on the guards of honour at Arlington National Cemetery, but razor-sharp ones. We regard North Korea as a threat because of its nuclear weapons, but they also have a million men under arms. If these swarms of zealous fighters were stretched out and unleashed across the border in such a way that fighter planes and machine gun emplacements were powerless to stop them, the South Korean capital would be overrun in days. The infantry poses a threat that no one appears to be aware of because we believe it is out of date.

In addition to my brother Lucki, another person experienced their first fantastic moment on Aguirre. This was Walter Saxer, a young Swiss from St. Gallen who had left home and met me on the Canary Island of Lanzarote while filming Even Dwarfs Started Small. He managed a tiny hotel on the island and assisted us in finding the automobile that was supposed to drive around in circles. Not long after we began filming, and the automobile, a rusted-out 1950s vehicle that appears in most of the footage, broke down irretrievably,

I believe it was the engine block. Within 24 hours, Saxer located a similar model on a country road, stopped it, and convinced the owner to sell his vehicle. He was handed a replacement, and Saxer spent the night modifying his old engine to fit our wreck. I'd never seen anything like it. Walter Saxer was simply indomitable. Nothing was too risky for him. He loathed anyone who didn't work as hard as he did, thus the performers' vanity often irritated him.

Walter Saxer was my production manager on Kaspar Hauser, Nosferatu the Vampyre, Woyzeck, Cobra Verde, and many more projects; he was involved in practically everything I did during those years. Fitzcarraldo was unquestionably his best achievement. The preparations lasted three and a half years. He initiated the construction of the two identical ships, which necessitated a complete infrastructure—in this case, a port in the middle of the jungle. He created camps for the teams of Indigenous extras and the technical crew, hired the extras, and brought the steamship up and over the mountain. One of our disagreements was that in interviews, I mentioned how I got the ship over the mountain when it was actually he and his crew who did it. In my conversations, I spoke figuratively—pars pro toto—about a man's motivation to hunt a white whale or lift a ship over a mountain. Let me clarify: in technical words, Walter Saxer carried the ship over the mountain. But I'd also like to mention that there was a crisis during the shoot when our Brazilian technician was terrified to drag the ship up the mountain because the prop—a deadpost known as muerto in Spanish—didn't appear stable enough to support it. I believe the Brazilian quit because he was terrified of his own courage. I then took responsibility and had a new muerto buried deep in the dirt. Technically, Saxer did it. This innovative prop could have supported the weight of five ships. Films are collaborative businesses; it is unfortunate that friendships do not always last, as Walter Saxer and I discovered.

Chapter 17: PRIVILEGIUM MAIUS, PITTSBURGH

By the age of 21, I had completed two short films and was determined to make a full-length feature. But at the time, it was unimaginable for a young guy to be tasked with such a responsibility. There was no one under the age of 35 in the profession anywhere. Several things came together at once. I was still earning money for my productions and doing sporadic stints at university. That was essentially false, but it provided me with some extra money in the form of a scholarship despite the fact that I was not learning anything. I had no time. I remember requesting a fellow student to write a term paper for me, and he did it effortlessly. In jest, he asked what I would do for him in return, and I jokingly vowed to make him eternal. His name is Hauke Stroszek. At a public ceremony in 2017, forty-five years after my time in Munich, when I received a European Film Award, a young woman introduced herself as my daughter. Hauke Stroszek had recently retired as a professor from a university in North Rhine-Westphalia. I gave his surname to the main character in my screenplay Signs of Fire, which was later filmed as Signs of Life in 1967. I later dubbed my second film Stroszek, which I made in 1976 with Bruno S. (more on whom later).

But there were some aspects of my study that I found extremely fascinating. For a mediaeval history lesson, I wrote a paper about the Privilegium Maius. This was a clear counterfeit dated 1358 or 1359; in fact, it was a collection of five mutually reinforcing forgeries, one allegedly dating back to Julius Caesar and Nero. This false title deed was about strengthening the influence of the rising Habsburgs, in this case Rudolf IV, and defining their region, which is nearly identical to that of modern Austria. The falsified documents resulted in the establishment of legally enforceable prerequisites and, ultimately, the formation of the state of Austria. The Renaissance poet Petrarch had previously detected the fabrication, but in historical terms, it was a triumph. It was an early case of fake news, and I developed a mechanism in my work that—unbeknownst to me—had never been utilised before. Because my films are still engaged with questions of factuality, reality, and truth, in the sense of what I like to refer to as "ecstatic truth," I will just provide a brief overview here. I declared, even if it was illogical, that the "privilegium" was a true account and knocked props into the ground to view the documents from all possible perspectives while always using a contemporary argumentation of the time—power politics, social change, understanding of the law, balance of military power—and at the end, one could remove the props and still have a supportable tissue of argument. In other words, falsification, or fake news, took on the structure of truth because history had rooted its alterations there, as in a developing truth.

What appeared to be a natural course of action drew notice. Because I realised it would be impossible to make a feature picture straight away, I took a scholarship to the United States—I barely had to apply for it. People were astonished that I wasn't a historian, but I was applying to a university with cameras and a film studio so that I could gain practical experience and further my development as a filmmaker. My early short films served as my only apprenticeship. I could have attended a more prominent university, but I chose Pittsburgh because I had a romantic belief that if I went there, I wouldn't be bogged down by academic jargon because I'd be in a city full of genuine down-to-earth workers. A few months later, at the age of twenty-two, I was awarded the prize of five thousand deutsche marks; but, because it had not been awarded the previous year, I was given ten thousand marks in 1964, which was the prize for both years. With it, I would be able to make another short film immediately. Every known and emerging director had competed; I recall Volker Schlöndorff, one of my opponents, with his Young Törless. Later on, that became an essential argument against film financiers who preferred to turn me down while backing the projects of others. I could refer to my screenplay being chosen over all others, as well as the fact that I had previously created films, which my competitors did not. Pittsburgh turned out to be a horrible idea; for starters, the steel industry was virtually dead; it was in steep decline, and the shuttered mills were rusting away; and second, Duquesne University, which housed the film studio, turned out to be an intellectually deprived place. I had no idea there were disparities amongst universities. Later, for various reasons, I grew to love and respect the city.

People didn't fly in the early 1960s, so I won another competition for a free Atlantic journey. I boarded the Bremen, where Siegfried and Roy had served as stewards the year before, distracting guests with magic shows before continuing to Las Vegas. My first wife, Martje, and I met on board this ship. After we reached the Irish Sea, it rained for a week, and the dining room for 800 passengers was empty after two days. There was one round table where the tough customers had departed their assigned seats to join their fellow walkers. Martje was on her way to Wisconsin to complete her literary degree. The rough waters did not worry her. We were more interested in playing shuffleboard on deck than in seeing the Statue of Liberty. Later, she finished her studies in Freiburg and we married. She is the mother of Rudolph, my first son. He is named after three people who have played significant roles in my life: Rudolph, Amos, and Achmed. Rudolph after my grandfather—oddly, I always thought his name finished with a ph, and it wasn't until I looked carefully for these memoirs that I realised it was Rudolf with a f. Amos is named after Amos Vogel, an American author, festival director, and film distributor who, like Lotte Eisner, served as a mentor to me. After almost three years of marriage, he took me aside and asked whether everything was okay. Of course it was fine. Despite ethnic cleansing following the Ottoman Empire's demise, he managed to remain on the now-Greek island. Achmed worked as a guard at the archeological digs at the Asklepieion on Cos, but every day he was subjected to martyrdom. When he lay out his prayer rug, the youngsters hurled stones at him, yelling, "Achmed! Achmed!" But he said his prayers and bore everything. There is a scene with him in my film Signs of Life. He had lost his wife, children, and even grandchild; all he had left by the time I encountered him again while working on the film was his dog, Bondchuk.

In Pittsburgh, I quickly realised that I was in the wrong area, and after a week, I knew I couldn't stay. There was a film studio, sure, but it was set up like a TV news studio, with a newscaster's desk flanked by three movable but highly heavy electronic cameras. Old-fashioned spotlights were fastened to the ceiling and could not be removed or moved. However, quitting school would have resulted in me losing my visa status and having to depart the United States straight away. So I kept my registration but cancelled my housing. A group of young writers gathered around a university journal, where I wrote my first short work. Everything seems blurry in my memory, as if events were layered on top of themselves. Sometimes I would sleep on the library floor, but that had a disadvantage because the cleaners would find me there at six a.m. I bounced between the sofas of several acquaintances and my original host, a forty-year-old professor who was afraid of his mother, who prevented him from interacting with female students and possibly women in general.

A random chance altered everything. My temporary home was at Fox Chapel, which was in the hills outside of Pittsburgh. I'd take the bus about twelve miles to Dorseyville, and then hike up the road through the woods. While walking the remaining mile, I observed that a woman in a car passed me many times. Usually, all of the chairs were filled with young people. It had begun to rain that day, and I was unprepared. The car pulled up next to me, and the woman rolled down her window; she could give me a ride; it wasn't hiking weather. The mother's name was Evelyn Franklin. She has six children aged seventeen to twenty-seven, and she felt a seventh would be ideal, given that her oldest daughter had recently married and moved out. So there was a vacancy in the group. Evelyn must have endured years of misery because her father died of alcoholism. She barely mentioned him in passing, always referring to him as Mr. Franklin. The youngest were twin girls, Jeannie and Joanie; then there was Billy, a failed rock musician; then two more brothers, one of whom—the only one!—was a little boring and bougie, and another, twenty-five, a little slow and with a soft heart, who some people considered mentally disabled. He had fallen out of a moving car as a child and had been slow ever since. Then there was a ninety-year-old grandmother and a cocker spaniel named Benjamin (after Benjamin Franklin). I was put in the attic, which had an old bed and other garbage. It had a sloped roof, and I could only stand upright in the centre, beneath the rooftree.

I immediately became a part of the daily craziness. Evelyn commuted to the city; she worked as a secretary for an insurance company. The twins returned from Fox Chapel High School in the afternoon, typically accompanied by friends. Long before that, starting at eight o'clock, the grandma would try to wake Billy, who had normally been rocking in some pub till three a.m. She would pound on his locked door every half hour or so, attempting to persuade him from his wicked lifestyle and reciting Bible verses to him. The dog, who had a symbiotic emotional link with Billy, lay despondently outside the door. In the afternoon, Billy would emerge completely naked, stretching with pleasure. The grandma would escape, leaving Billy to smite his chest and lament his sinful life in Old Testament tones. Benjamin Franklin howled in response, but knowing what was coming next, he kicked his back paws in the air. Billy switched into an imaginary canine language and began dragging Benjamin Franklin down the stairs by his back paws, similar to how Christopher Robin carried Winnie-the-Pooh below behind him. At each carpeted landing, he paused to mourn his wicked scrapes in canine language. Down in the living room, the twins and their giggling girlfriends escaped the naked youth, who was now pursuing his fleeing grandmother. Billy now delivered his jeremiads in a combination of Old Testament prophet and cocker spaniel.

The twins setting off after me, squirting me with Woolworth's eau de parfum, was not unusual in this crazy creative environment. They were full of ideas. One day, I noticed them planning an ambush for me behind the door leading down to the garage, so I crept into the top-floor bathroom, meaning to leap all the way down and attack them from behind as they passed through the garage. My personal preferred weapon was shaving foam. It had snowed, but there was only about an inch of loose snow, which I believed was adequate padding for my leap. I fell on the spiral concrete stairway leading down to the garage. My ankle made a penetrating sound that I can still hear now, similar to a wet branch snapping when stepped on. The fracture was so severe that I had to be operated on and placed in a plaster cast that extended up to my hip. After a month, I was given a walking cast that only extended up to my knee.

I adored the Franklins. With them, I learned about some of America's most profound and positive aspects. Later, I invited them to Munich and brought them to Sachrang for a village celebration. Hugs, beer, squeals, and whoops. I led them up the Geigelstein. Contact became more difficult in subsequent years as the entire family, including Billy, turned to fundamentalism. When I saw them, I could not recognize them because they'd all gained so much weight. When I was cast as the villain in the 2012 Hollywood action thriller Jack Reacher, both the director, Christopher McQuarrie, and the actor, Tom Cruise, wanted me. The filming took place in Pittsburgh. But I couldn't find the Franklins anymore; they had scattered to the four winds. I drove out to Fox Chapel. Almost everything in the neighbourhood had changed; there were new buildings everywhere, which was really dismal. The house on Oak Spring Drive remained almost identical; the yard included the same old broad-leaved trees, but the path down to the garage was overgrown with flowering bushes. No one was home. I tried various neighbours, met an old couple, and discovered that the house had changed hands multiple times. I knew Evelyn Franklin had died. A year later, I learned that Billy had also died; he was like another brother to me. We discovered our relationship almost immediately.

The twins and their girlfriends were ecstatic that a new British band would be performing at the Civic Arena. They were known as the Rolling Stones. So far, I'd missed out on all of these acts and pop culture in general. The only exception was Elvis, whose first picture I'd watched in Munich, and the kids all around me began calmly and deliberately tearing the place apart. I recall the police being summoned. Now in Pittsburgh, the twins brought a piece of cardboard to the concert with the name of their favourite, Brian, written on it. He was their front man at the time; not long after, he was discovered dead in his swimming pool. I remember being astounded by the ruckus and the girls' screams. When the event ended, I saw that many of the plastic bucket seats were steaming. Many of the girls had pissed themselves. When I saw that, I knew it was going to be huge. Much later, in Fitzcarraldo, Mick Jagger played the second role alongside Jason Robards, but Robards became ill, and filming was halted halfway through. Everything would have to be done again, this time with Klaus Kinski. Mick Jagger's role was so unusual and one-of-a-kind that I didn't want to recast it, so I cut it entirely from the script. I only had him on contract for three more weeks since the Stones were about to embark on a world tour with all of the dates set. He was supposed to play Wilbur in my film, an English actor who had lost his mind and ended up in the Amazon. The character owes something to the stark-naked Billy Franklin of Pittsburgh. McNamara, a timid ape, played the role of Benjamin Franklin, the dog.

Chapter 18: NASA, MEXICO

I obtained a job working as a producer for WQED in Pittsburgh. His name was Matt, short for Matthias von Brauchitsch, a relative of the former field marshal and commander-in-chief of the German army, who fell out of favour with Hitler in 1941. I kept quiet about the fact that I did not have a work permit. Von Brauchitsch was working on many documentaries for NASA regarding future rocket fuel choices. I had no training or references, but he felt confident in my abilities. Even now, I appreciate the United States for its realistic optimism. The film I was to make for him was on early theoretical research on plasma rockets, which was mostly conducted in Cleveland, Ohio. Simply put, superheated plasma was intended to be utilised as fuel, but the temperatures would have melted any solid container, therefore the experiment focused on nonmaterial containers made from incredibly intense magnetic fields. The most powerful magnet in existence at the time was located in Cleveland. Right adjacent to it was an experimental atomic reactor. I recall passageways with open doors and mathematicians working in vacant rooms. The near catastrophe led to the hall being locked down immediately and the situation being examined. As a result, more stringent security procedures were implemented, necessitating further security clearance for everyone there, which led to my departure from the project and the end of my time in the States.

My involvement in this cinematic project was later subject to extensive distortion. I'd been making films for NASA. I formerly worked as a scientist for NASA. I'd abandoned my career as a scientist and possible astronaut in favour of a cinematic career. All of these inventions seem excellent and do not concern me. They do not worry me since I understand who I am. Or, more specifically, there are areas where memory creates itself, takes on new shapes, and spreads over the sleepwalker like a delicate veil.

Ten days after the event in the vacuum room, I received a summons from immigration. I had to introduce myself immediately and carry my passport. I understood what that meant. Because I had breached the terms of my visa, I was going to be deported not just across the border, but all the way to Germany. In Pittsburgh, I hurriedly purchased a Spanish dictionary and drove away. The separation from the Franklins was terrible, but we knew we'd see each other again somewhere. I drove practically nonstop to Texas, crossing the border in Laredo. In the no-man's land on the bridge over the Rio Grande, something grinds in my VW engine, as if the United States didn't want to let me leave and Mexico wasn't quite ready to accept me. I pushed the car into Mexico for repairs. Two days later, I continued on, prepared to face whatever came my way. First, I stopped in Guanajuato to work for the charreadas, but that ended after a few weekends due to an unexpected occurrence.

I needed an additional source of money. I began bringing stereos and television sets across the border for a few wealthy rancheros I met at the charreadas. These items were substantially more expensive in Mexico due to the duty. I was able to do so because there was a border gap between Reynosa and McAllen. Day labourers arrived in McAllen in the morning and left at night for Mexico. Three lanes of the enlarged route were reserved for them, and their vehicles were recognizable by windshield stickers. Mexicans received such stickers only after passing through security inspections by US authorities. I managed to obtain several Mexican plates and one of the stickers. My beat-up old automobile looked the part. Early in the morning, the US Border Patrol casually waved me through on the special lanes alongside a few thousand other automobiles. It sounds ridiculous now, but there was minimal drug smuggling in 1965, and gang battles had not even begun. Anyone who wished to enter the United States illegally swam over the Rio Grande and arrived on the other side as a mojado. The only thing I was concerned about was getting into McAllen without the Border Patrol inspecting the visa in my passport. On the way back, the Mexicans simply waved you in. In a few cases, I imported Colt revolvers into Mexico, which were essentially ornamental weapons with mother-of-pearl inlay handles.

I moved inland to San Miguel de Allende, a lovely small colonial town that has been absolutely spoiled. Around the time I was there, the first wave of artists had begun to settle, and over the decades, they would attract large numbers of confused and rich Americans, all eager to connect with their talent. I find it difficult to set foot there right now. However, on my subsequent excursions, I discovered the Guanajuato mummies, which were at the time arranged in long rows against a wall. My picture Nosferatu, which I made twelve years later, begins with a long sequence of those mummies, all of them had their mouths open as if screaming. By the time I returned to film, the mummies had been relocated to a museum and displayed in long glass cases. We were able to remove them from their glass coffins and prop them against a wall in the dead of night. I'll never forget how light they were, like paper, when all the liquid had been emptied out of them. The opening of that film is not about symbolism, or only somewhat so. I had seen the mummies, and they became a part of me.

All this time, I had been working on my film project, Signs of Life. Back in Munich, my mother was constantly mailing applications to film funding committees and sending out copies of my early films for watching. I knew I'd have to go home eventually. Then I got sick in southern Mexico, near the Guatemalan border. It was hepatitis, but I didn't know. I wasn't awarded a visa to Guatemala, but I was preoccupied with the vague idea of assisting in the formation of an independent Mayan state in Petén. The news of this initiative had reached me. I remember the asphalt road through the jungle, where many snakes had been run over, as well as the clean waters and large stones where ladies were washing their clothes.

I was secretly happy that I hadn't made it across the border. It was also becoming evident to me that I was unwell. I felt miserable and feverish. I drove back to Texas practically without stopping, this time without false plates or a windshield sticker. There wasn't any electronic data yet, and I figured I'd be able to return to the nation on my exchange student visa. What was I doing in Mexico? I claimed to be on a brief research trip and was permitted back in. From that point forward, everything is a feverish fog. I travelled all day and night, stopping only briefly to rest my weary head on the passenger seat for a few hours. I recall a village on a Native American reserve in Cherokee, North Carolina. I went for gas and ate a cheeseburger prepared by a Native American woman. Her clothing resembled something you would see at a carnival. Years later, I returned, and the dancing chickens in my 1976 film Stroszek are most likely the wildest thing I've ever presented on screen. When I see the film's ending section now, I can see those hens as if they were hallucinations from my drive. I made it to Pittsburgh. The Franklins took me to the hospital right away. After a few weeks, they came to pick me up, all of them. After two further days, I travelled back to Germany.

Chapter 19: PURA VIDA

I accept that I can no longer hop with my right foot. It was a foolish thing that happened when I jumped out of the window, but in Mexico, one of the men in the arena, a famous lasso master, convinced me that this was part of life, pura vida. His name was Euklides. He shook my hand the first time I was thrown, gushing from my mouth because I nearly bit off my tongue when I struck the deck. His hand felt like a vise. He did not mean the purity of life, as the early saints did, but rather the sheer, physical, unpredictable, and overwhelming presence of life. In his memory, I later gave his name to a crippled twelve-year-old who manages a guesthouse in my 1987 film Cobra Verde and is the only one who is not terrified of the bandit of that name, played by Klaus Kinski.

I was able to continue playing soccer in Germany because my jumping foot is naturally on the left. My brother Till brought me to Munich Black-Yellow, where I played either goalkeeper or centre forward. The other members of the squad were taxi drivers, bakers, and office workers, and I adored them all. Black-Yellow did not compete in any of the official leagues, but we may have held our own in the fifth. My brother was a better goalkeeper than I was. When he was fourteen, he grabbed the attention of a talent scout from 1860 Munich, the dominant local team prior to the birth of Bayern Munich, but my mother persuaded him not to pursue a career in professional sports. Sepp Mosmeir, a pastry chef, founded Black-Yellow, and I have never encountered a more charming man. Sepp exuded unconditional warmth, adored opera, and possessed exceptional leadership abilities. We'd do everything for him. However, there was a shadow over him as well. When he was growing up in South Tyrol, he and his pals climbed an electrical pole along a railway line, and one of them grabbed the power line. The youngster trembled for several minutes, and smoke began to come out of him. Sepp reported the sound that occurred as the boy's burnt body finally touched the ground. It sounded like a sack of briquettes hitting the gravel ballast under the rails.

When we were kids in Wüstenrot, we had a war with newly hulled chestnuts, and I climbed up on the roof of a barn to be safe and observe where the other kids were hiding. I was seated on the gable when I heard my name shouted. I turned toward the voice, and a missile struck me in the eye. A lightning bolt struck me, and I recall tumbling down the steep roof to my front. I fell headfirst into a pile of farm gear far below me; I can still see the iron rods and blades. My forearm fractures both bones. The doctor at Wüstenrot failed to properly set the break. After a week of intense suffering, the cast was removed and everything was reset.

My worst experience, however, was a skiing accident near Avoriaz and Mont Blanc. I'd been invited to screen a film at the festival and had borrowed some skis. I was drawn to a breath-takingly steep hill where several athletes were attempting the ridiculous feat of breaking the ski speed record, which stood at 220 km/h at the time. For high speeds, the racers wore lengthy aerodynamic helmets that reached their tailbones and a kind of spoiler on their calves. After my party had left, I remained behind and surveyed the slope. Finally, I went down around two-thirds of it. The mood was thrilling. A slight climb on the opposite side helped you slow down at the bottom. That evening, I discussed what I'd done, and everyone laughed since I assumed I'd gone at least 140 km/h. I recall two things: on my skis, I was raced by my brother Lucki and an Israeli producer, Arnon Milchan, both towering guys, at eye level; at that point, I realised I was too high. I can see myself landing on the slope in slow motion; one of my skis flew away like a spear. Lucki still can't express what he witnessed. But my ski boot got trapped in the snow, and I fell over headfirst. I must have been catapulted many yards into the air on the steep hill, and I came to a stop approximately a hundred yards later. The most imminent risk was that I'd choke on my vomit. When I

73

returned, I noticed blood and vomit in the snow and heard someone sigh gently. I go into such detail because I am ashamed of the accident and, in some ways, a result of my blunders and misjudgments.

In 1998, I sent two trips into the woods along the Pachitea River, but they returned empty-handed. Then I located one of the three forest workers who had rescued Juliane. He had a good memory of the location and headed out on his own to discover it. Going up the small Shebonya River, he stepped on a stingray hidden under sand and shallow water, and its tail slashed through several layers of rubber on the heel of his boot. These rays are extremely toxic, more fatal than most snakes. He lay dying on a sandbank for two days before being discovered by a canoe. The paddlers first refused to accompany him since he did not have enough money to compensate them. Finally, he handed over his gun as payment, and they pulled him into their canoe. In this manner, he was saved. I discovered the canoeists and purchased the gun from them. Juliane presents it to him in the film as a gift after meeting her saving angel for the first time in years. He also led the fourth mission to investigate the crash site. The wreckage had not been transported; only the bodies and body parts had been gathered.

Later, my assistant Herb Golder was dropped to the location via a steel cable; he was accompanied by several woodsmen who cut down a few trees so we could land a helicopter. That location served as the shoot's base camp. My pal Herb Golder assisted me on several films. In my film Invincible, he plays a believable Rabbi. I tested dozens of actors, and Herb was the only one who could portray the scenario with conviction and intelligence. Later, we collaborated on a narrative he had been investigating for years, My Son, My Son, What Have Ye Done, which was released in 2009. Herb currently works as a classics professor at Boston University. I don't know anyone with whom I can have such in-depth discussions on ancient history.

However, Herb is more than just a bookworm. He's built like an oak and holds black belts in several martial arts. When he opens his mouth, lazy extras stop reclining and raise their ears. I ended up making the picture in 2008 with Michael Shannon, the most talented actor of his generation.

Chapter 20: DANCE ON THE WIRE

Many aspects of my life appear to me to be a high-wire act, despite the fact that I am usually unaware of the abysses on either side of me. It's no surprise that I'm acquainted with Philippe Petit, who rose to prominence when, shortly before the World Trade Center opened in New York, he stretched a wire between the Twin Towers and danced his way over at dizzying heights. He had looked for me and found me when Signs of Life was exhibited at a film festival in New York City. His walk to the Twin Towers had been planned for quite some time. He had just carried out a stealthy coup in Savoy, Europe's deepest canyon. using the Twin structures, he had infiltrated a team of welders using bogus papers years previously and even formed a construction company to gain a footing in one of the unfinished structures. He progressively built a storeroom in his office for the steel wire and other components he required. He then launched an arrow from one of the flat roofs at the twin structure, which was hooked to a fishing line. He went out on the rope around six a.m. He was unconcerned; no one observed or watched him until 410 metres below him, a cab driver appeared to look up. A traffic congestion formed, stretching several blocks northward. Police swarmed both roofs, but they were unable to free Philippe from his rope. Finally, he lay flat on it to sleep, as a police helicopter was dangerously churning up the air.

Philippe then opened a manhole cover and escorted me into his secret world of subterranean tunnels and rooms in Paris late at night. Thousands of corpses were neatly stacked in one large cavern, while skulls from the Black Death could be found in another. Another night, we set out with sixty yards of climbing rope and a hook; Philippe intended to explore the roof of the Gothic church of St. Eustache in Les Halles, but we were interrupted by a famous singer and actor on his intoxicated journey home, so we abandoned our goal. When I launched the 1991 Viennale festival in Vienna, I had

Philippe walk between the antiaircraft gun tower and the Apollo cinema's tower.

I may not have noticed the chasms along the route, but as if dogged by a curse, I appeared to attract disaster while working on my projects. Everything was ready for my debut feature film, Signs of Life, when the Greek military conducted their coup. Then, all of a sudden, rail connections failed, flights ceased to operate, and no one knew what had occurred. I was unable to contact anyone, so I travelled from Munich to Athens almost nonstop. The border was still open. The ministry in charge of film approvals was closed, and troops were sleeping in the corridors. Our Greek production director informed me that all existing approvals had been revoked, and I could see for myself that, while the junta was interested in a variety of things, it was not interested in international film production.

That was only the beginning of our issues.We had to break up two weeks before the shoot's intended conclusion date. My actor spent six months in the hospital and rehab before we could resume production. Even after that, Brogle required a sophisticated piece of equipment linked to his hip to walk. We could only film him from the waist up, and we hadn't yet shot the scene on Crete with all the windmills. Then Thomas Mauch came up with a simple but great idea: he videotaped an extra's boots and legs mounting the rough terrain, while Brogle stood by to continue his strides. As the camera pans upward, it temporarily leaves the legs to capture the character's upper torso and face before following him to the edge of the terrain, where many thousand windmills await.

The films listed below were all similarly impacted. Before we even crossed into Africa, the cameraman Jörg Schmidt-Reitwein got his finger stuck in some machinery, causing the bone to break into fragments that had to be strung on a steel wire. Then we were imprisoned in Cameroon, for reasons I still do not understand. We were on our way from there to the interior of the Rwenzori

Mountains, which border Congo and Uganda, but my cameraman and I were ill in the Central African Republic and were unable to travel. We had to halt the shoot in Bangui to acquire additional footage for the next two films. In Even Dwarfs Started Small, fate smiled on us, and we had nothing but good fortune. That film depicts a rebellion at an institution in which the inmates destroy everything. All of the objects were regular size to us, but because the performers were so small, things like a motorcycle or a double bed were huge.

The majority of Errol's interactions were up and down. He had spent months in a godforsaken hole called Plainfield, Wisconsin, conducting study on serial killers. Plainfield was where the most notorious of all American murders, Ed Gein, operated. Hitchcock's Psycho was inspired by him. Aside from his killings, in which he gutted his victims like deer and used their skin for lampshades and sofa coverings, Gein had a tendency of discreetly digging newly buried bodies. Errol noted that the opened graves formed a ring, with Gein's mother's grave in the centre. Did Ed Gein also excavate his mother? We debated this subject for quite some time. Errol's only means of receiving a definitive answer was to surreptitiously dig her up himself. If his mother's body was still there, he hadn't; if it was gone, he had. I offered to help him. In a few months, I'd be travelling from New York to Alaska to film, and halfway there, I planned to meet Errol on such and such a date. I arrived in Plainfield with shovels and pickaxes, but Errol had lost his courage. He'd disappeared. My vain wait in Plainfield had one advantage. The car was having gearbox issues, but there was no technician in Plainfield. A few miles away, there was a junkyard with a technician salvaging automobiles for parts. I was enthralled by the location and its owner, and a year later, I returned and persuaded the mechanic to portray one of the main characters in my film Stroszek. The junkyard and the bleak flatness all around it were ideal for depicting what happened to the American Dream.

Fitzcarraldo suffered the brunt of fate's strikes. Whenever I'm on a really difficult shoot, I always bring Luther's 1545 translation of the Bible in facsimile reprint with me. I find comfort in the Book of Job and the Psalms. I also have Livy's account of the Second Punic War, which lasted from 218 to 201 BC and began with Hannibal's departure from North Africa and his crossing of the Alps with elephants, an incredible feat of courage. After terrible setbacks at Lake Trasimene and Cannae, Rome was on the verge of ruin. In that almost hopeless situation, Quintus Fabius Maximus was given command and saved Rome, and hence most likely the West as we know it, which would otherwise have been Phoenician rather than Roman. His strategy was to retreat indefinitely, never willing to fight. Because it would have been the end.

Fitzcarraldo's preparations lasted more than three years. Originally, 20th Century Fox planned to make the movie. Jack Nicholson was impressed by my films and wanted to play the lead, but it quickly became evident that he and 20th Century Fox planned to shoot the feature in San Diego's botanical gardens, using a plastic scale replica of the ship. We didn't have the modern digital box of tricks back in the early 1980s. Also, Nicholson only took the bits that allowed him to watch Los Angeles Lakers games. He flew me to one in Denver on his private plane and attempted to persuade me that the San Diego approach was the simplest. In retrospect, I'm astonished at how many actors were considered; another was Warren Oates, who would have been interesting—cast against type—as Fitzcarraldo. He had a squishy "proletarian" face and was most recognized for his roles in The Wild Bunch and Alfredo Garcia's Bring Me The Head. There were ships to build and jungle camps to set up, but at a large meeting of all the participants, including lawyers, the representatives of 20th Century Fox were quite polite and addressed me by my first name.

Later, I was repeatedly asked why I hadn't made the film near the Peruvian jungle city of Iquitos, with its hotels and airport, i.e., in a more accessible jungle area. However, the land around Iquitos is so flat for the next three thousand kilometres that the height difference with the Atlantic is only approximately a hundred metres. In contrast, we were looking for a location with two parallel Amazon tributaries separated by a short mountain range. But this didn't seem to exist anyplace. The rivers in the jungle typically flow in parallel, but they are 25 miles apart, and the mountains are far too high. At the confluence of the Río Marañón and the Río Cenepa, we discovered an oxbow bend on the Cenepa that was near the Marañón. There was a barrier that was only 100 metres tall. The ship, still under construction, would be hoisted from the Cenepa into the Marañón. The Marañón merges with Santiago a short distance downstream. The joined rivers then break through a range of mountains. The water course narrows in a gorge, forming the infamous Pongo de Manseriche rapids, which can be particularly dangerous at high water. I kept a diary at the time, which I published years later under the title Conquest of the Useless.

We'd made an agreement with the adjoining village of Wawaim. However, there were political conflicts between two opposing camps of Aguaruna towns, and one of the groups, located thirty kilometres downstream, took advantage of our presence to raise their profile. Given the situation, I evacuated the whole crew from the camp, leaving only a medical station to serve the locals. Aguarunas occupied the camp and took advantage of the disarray to burn it down. They'd invited reporters to witness it. I was in Iquitos and heard radio transmissions from the camp that were crackly and difficult to understand. I recorded everything on a tape machine so I could figure out what was going on in peace. But I recognized that it meant, for the time being, the end of production.

It became worse. The Peruvian and international media accused me of destroying the locals' fields during filming, imprisoning some of the Aguarana people, violating their human rights, and a variety of other rubbish. There was a public tribunal against me in Germany, which seemed to cast a pall over the film. At the moment, Volker Schlöndorff was the only person who really supported me. I recall a press conference at the Filmfest Hamburg in front of a large crowd of journalists, where I was presenting documents that unequivocally confirmed my viewpoint, when Schlöndorff abruptly stepped to the front. His face was purple; I assumed he'd had a seizure. But he yelled at the media so loudly that I wondered where this slight man obtained such a powerful voice. He is the only director of the New German Cinema with whom I share a personal friendship. Amnesty International confirmed that four Aguarunas were detained by police in Santa María de Nieva prior to the shooting for unrelated reasons, including unpaid bills from local bar owners and shopkeepers.

Every conceivable disaster, not just film catastrophes, but actual catastrophes, struck me. When my lead, Jason Robards, became ill halfway through the shoot and we had to fly him back to the States, it was only a "film catastrophe." Then his physicians refused to let him go back into the woods. We had to reshoot, this time with Kinski in the major role and my brother Lucki keeping the collapsing production together. He called all of the financial backers and insurers to a meeting in Munich and told them the truth. He then explained his rescue strategy. He rescued the production. I was questioned if I still had enough strength to reshoot the film. I stated that if this project failed, all of my dreams would come to an end, and I did not want to live as a man without dreams.

Just two days later, we captured footage of the unmanned ship—one of two identical twins—being catapulted through the Pongo de Mainique rapids. It bounced off the rocks on either side with such power that I saw the camera's lens fly out. I tried to grab on to the photographer, Thomas Mauch, but we flew after the lens, and he hit the deck with the heavy camera still in his hand. The force of the crash ripped the webbing between his two final fingers deep into his palm. He, too, was stitched up by our gifted Indigenous assistant paramedic, who was extremely skilled at dislocating and stitching up wounds and had once put Mauch's dislocated shoulder back, but because all of the anaesthetics had been used up in the hour-long operations on the arrow victims and couldn't be replaced for some time, Mauch suffered greatly. I held him in my arms, but it did not help much. Finally, I summoned Carmen, one of the two working females we had hired, who pressed his head against her breasts and spoke sweetly to him. She did so lovingly, magnanimously, and valiantly. Even the Dominican priest from the missionary station at Timpia, fifty kilometres downriver, insisted on having prostitutes in our company because, with the number of male woodcutters and canoeists, there was a high risk of attacks on the local population. These types of events appeared to occur frequently. We had to deal with the most violent rainy season in sixty-five years, which obviously had an enormous impact on labour and camp supplies via tiny planes landing on tiny mud airstrips; Walter Saxer himself took huge risks. The rivers rose to incredible heights, sweeping away bushes and tree limbs, and sometimes entire islands of massive trunks. You couldn't run a motorboat or land a seaplane on them. Then the water level dropped so dramatically that we couldn't move the ship back off the mountain into the Urubamba, where the average water level was eight metres but was now fifty centimetres. We could begin the work only six months later. This was accentuated by personal bewilderment and a strong sense of loneliness because, after weeks of being unable to carry the ship up the slope, practically everyone discreetly abandoned the endeavour. Being alone has never worried me; but, being alone among a crowd of people who had given up on me and questioned my sanity was challenging. Lucki was one of the few people who maintained their beliefs. My diary entries in my ever-shrinking script appeared to become indecipherable and minuscule, then stopped for nearly a year in the forest, the year of hardships. However, I was always ready to confront everyone and everyone, no matter what job or life threw at me.

Chapter 21: MENHIRS AND THE VANISHING AREA PARADOX

One of the essential events occurred by chance while I was seeking for a windswept coast to set a dream sequence in Kaspar Hauser eight years earlier, in 1974. Among the choices were the Lofoten Islands and Norway's northern shore, but because they were so far away, I began driving down the coast of Brittany. One evening, as darkness fell, I stopped in a parking lot in Carnac and noticed something beautiful in my headlights. Thousands of Neolithic stones were lined up in long rows uphill and down, like soldiers emerging from the void. In the darkness, I found my way down the rows of menhirs before crawling into the car to sleep. The next morning, I strolled across the parallel rows of chiselled blocks. I purchased a guide at the ticket booth, where I read the ridiculous claim that transporting these stones would have been impossible for men thousands of years ago, and thus they could only have been placed there by extraterrestrial visitors from another galaxy.

That same day, I devised a plan to use solely primitive technology: shovels, ropes, stone axes, animal grease as a lubricant, and fire. For the purpose of simplicity, I posed the question to myself as follows: I assumed I had a massive stone already hewn among the countless rocks on this coast and that I needed to move it half a mile on the flat and place it somewhere. With the assistance of a thousand disciplined men, I could complete it in a year. The key job would be to construct a sturdy, half-mile-long ramp that was close to level. Even with a half-percent incline, the ramp would be five metres tall by the end. At that point, I would make a tiny hill and drill a massive crater into it. The massive stone would be tunnelled beneath crosswise at the start of the transportation procedure, with round fire-hardened oak logs shoved into the tunnels. When the rest of the dirt was removed, the block would rest on rollers. Moving it would be simple—it would be on wheels, so to speak. Finally, the menhir would tumble into the crater hole of the earthen hill, and all that remained was to shovel the hill's earth away, leaving a bit at the base for stability.

It would be more difficult on sloping terrain, such here at Carnac. However, the same notion of a fixed ramp and a crater would work here as well, only that moving the stone uphill would require slightly more strength. To do this, I would utilise a turnstile mechanism, winding a rope from a fixed trunk or pole to apply energy to distance; I would turn the huge cross and wind the rope on a spindle. A number of such turnstiles should be sufficient to transport at least one hundred tons up a slope. Fitzcarraldo exemplified this philosophy. Machiguengas press against the turnstiles' long arms, while on the ground, a hawser is looped around a post.

In 1999, when directing The Magic Flute in Catania, I had Maurizio Balò, a talented set designer, create a background set depicting enslaved Egyptians raising an obelisk. The libretto for The Magic Flute is set in fantasy pharaonic Egypt, thus I needed a visual representation of the setting. The obelisk is erected in my creation using rollers and turnstiles. Then, a few years ago, I came across a set of engravings depicting the creation of an obelisk in St. Peter's Square in Rome in 1586. I was amazed. There was a ramp and many, many turnstiles, the difference being that they were powered by horsepower and that pulleys and hoists were utilised to manage the large number of ropes. I was so interested by this revelation that I was granted access to the Vatican library to see the files on the obelisk's erection.

The enormous menhir at Locmariaquer in Brittany appears to confirm my theory that in prehistoric times, they must have employed the hollow hill approach for situating a menhir. This stone is by far the largest of its kind. Standing upright, it must have been over twenty metres tall and weighed at least 330 tons. It was probably raised in the fifth or sixth millennia BCE. It is now in four pieces on the ground, although it is unlikely that it shattered on the ground because the largest and heaviest piece is lying in one direction and the other three are some distance away, pointing somewhere else. Speculation concerning it is hazy and inconsistent. My hypothesis is as follows: when the stone was dropped into the crater hole of the man-made hill, the top third broke off due to the sheer weight of the impact, most likely against the crater's lip, resulting in a calculated breaking point. Perhaps there were pre existing cracks in the stone. When a cat leaps out of a third-floor window, it is unharmed; an elephant in a zoo can be discouraged from fleeing by a three-foot-deep concrete trench since the animal's hefty limb bones would be broken due to the inertia of its massive size. As a result, the top of the stone splintered against the hill's angle into three halves, each pointing in the same direction.

Engineers had disassembled the ship, which weighed approximately thirty tons, in the midst of the bush and transported it to a parallel river, where it was reconstructed. I had Joe sit down again. Everything started to make sense in my head: fever dreams in the forest, a three-hundred-ton steamship transported over a mountain, turnstiles manned by Indigenous peoples to wind it up as it was done in the Stone Age, Caruso's voice, great opera in the jungle. When I disembarked from a flight in the sweltering heat of Iquitos and saw vultures hovering overhead and pigs wallowing in mud right next to the landing strip—one of them was decaying; it had been hit by a plane—I recoiled automatically. Oh, gosh, not another film like that! But this endeavour, like the others, blew me away. I had no choice. I say this because it is generally considered that I am obsessive. In fact, I risked everything I had to get the project started. After a very short time, I was living in a converted chicken coop with a papier-mâché ceiling that was only slightly higher than the top of my head. In Iquitos' Indigenous market, I traded my shampoo and soap for three kilos of rice, which I used to feed myself for the next three weeks. I accepted essentials and little else, and felt it as my responsibility to pursue a huge goal.

I don't like accepting things as given. This is how I see the so-called vanishing area paradox. In my dentist's waiting room in Los Angeles, I once leafed through Scientific American, a serious and well-respected monthly. On one of its pages, a graphic depicted a conundrum that defied logic and experience. Sixteen distinct elements form a pattern that, when assembled in a different order, results in a blank in the centre of the same plane. I ripped out the page since my name was called at that exact moment. I intended to settle the issue on my own.

In my 2020 film Fireball, there is a sequence of quasiperiodic crystals discovered in shards of a meteorite that fell in Siberia near the Bering Strait. Crystals have rigorous symmetries; this has been understood for two centuries or more; anything different is unimaginable and prohibited. However, in the 1970s, British mathematician Roger Penrose developed a type of geometry that demonstrated the unthinkable. The most astounding thing is that in 1453, some Persian craftsmen built a quasiperiodic arrangement of tiles on the outside wall of an Isfahan shrine without understanding the mathematics behind such a pattern. I met Penrose and now have even more respect for the unthinkable. But I was interested by Scientific American's description of the vanishing area issue as intractable. After all, Aristotle had not been questioned for two millennia simply because he was Aristotle.

After much thought about the problem, I abandoned geometrical reasoning. I approached the dilemma in a different way because it contradicted everything of my real-world experience. The paradox was not a paradox; it was a fraud. The sum of the minor enlargements and reductions in the area was exactly the size of the small rectangle in the second graph. It took me two months to get there, while others could have done it in minutes. Consider the amount of time you might spend waiting for your dentist.

Chapter 22: THE BALLAD OF THE LITTLE SOLDIER

Fitzcarraldo was a difficult, wild ride, with moments, music, and interludes that I was still absorbing long after the filming was completed. In 1984, the two ascended Gasherbrum I one way and descended another, eventually arriving at the foot of Gasherbrum II. They climbed up and over this as well, and we waited for them at their base camp. The achievement was outstanding. It was groundbreaking, as was nearly everything Messner did. I am convinced that he is the most important climber not only of our time, but of all time. Messner's expertise and Kammerlander's personal warmth formed an excellent character mix in the picture. The Dark Glow of the Mountains was finished in 1985. But what I had in mind was a major film to be shot on K2 on the route to the Gasherbrum Mountains. For the final fifty miles, you'll follow the enormous stream of the Baltoro Glacier, into which a glacier flows from K2. I dreamed about K2 because it is so solitary and spectacular, similar to the Matterhorn in the Swiss Alps, except that the world's second tallest mountain is the most perilous by far.

The shooting ended when the two mountaineers went off into the black night with their headlamps and were nothing more than tiny fading specks the next day, vanished from view. A few days later, a Spanish expedition that was camping next to us offered to accompany them on a trip up Gasherbrum since they had failed to reach the top and wanted to remove their higher camp. Then I discovered I had the telltale indicators of early altitude sickness. One hint was that I sat in the snow while the Spaniards dismantled their camp, and eventually, feeling increasingly apathetic, I lay down on my back. At that point, I realised I needed to reduce altitude. The Spaniards took my word for it and released me. It should never have been permitted to occur. I set out by myself; visibility was fine. There is, however, the unbreakable requirement that at least one other man must accompany you for safety on the rope. When I reached the upper limit of the ice break, I opted to go around it. Something similar happened to Kammerlander toward the end of their long climb, but he was attached to Messner with a vine cable. To conserve weight, the two men didn't bring normal mountaineering rope, but the cord was enough to save Kammerlander from falling into the nothingness. In my situation, the Spanish were embarrassed by their oversight subsequently. I already had a storyline for my film on K2, a type of science fiction idea involving a radar station on an almost inaccessible peak, but after my own experiences on Gasherbrum, that project was abandoned because I always listened to the voice of caution.

In 1983, I was in Australia prepping for my film, Where the Green Ants Dream. This time, the subject was a battle between a group of Aboriginal people preserving one of their holy sites and a mining company's bulldozers; it is also about the last speakers of a dying language and complicated myths. It became evident to me that starting from my own culture, I would never be able to grasp Aboriginal minds and their concept of dreamtime, so I created my own tale of green ants, which is depicted in the video. I had met Michael and seen several of his films in Cannes in 1976, and I requested him to play a cameo in Nosferatu. Walter Saxer, costume designer Gisela Storch, and Anja Schmidt-Zäringer, a faithful and smart long-term collaborator of mine, are all in the same scene, inviting Isabelle Adjani to a feast in the open. Thousands of rats are milling at their feet.

When Denis Reichle approached me to direct a film for him about child soldiers in Nicaragua, I had to decline because I was too immersed in my new project in the Australian Outback. My challenge over those months, among others, was that I wanted to shoot four hundred thousand ants standing still and mysteriously waving their antennae. I wanted them all to face the same way, like iron filings in a tremendous magnetic field. I collaborated with cryobiologists, but our experiments were ineffective. In the end, I had to cut the sequence, so the ants did not materialise; they were simply mentioned. What is not practicable, I will not accomplish.

The following day, there was supposed to be an attack on a Sandinista camp staged for the cameras, but Denis and I were against any fight scenes that were solely for show. He coldly approached the commander, who was a pretentious son of a bitch, and inquired about the helicopter in the opposing camp. "There was no helicopter," the comandante responded. Denis questioned how he knew that. It turns out that it was just guesswork and wishful thinking. The obvious hazard in an attack was that if the soldiers retreated, there would be a mile of open grassland with little protection until they reached the jungle's edge. Denis inquired as to who would man the machine gun nests on the dirt road leading from the camp to our location in the event of an attack, as well as who would man the position on the opposite side, where an attack could also occur. A single machine gun, manned by two men, could easily pin down an entire truckload of soldiers until our side reached safety. The comandante had never heard of such an approach. But he gave himself all kinds of airs anyhow; he claimed to have slain numerous guys mano a mano and was about to do so again. He immediately ordered the retreat while still bragging about his courage.

The small warriors made a strong impression on me. These children dragged into conflict are more real to me than many of the people I've known in my life. Sometimes I wonder if there isn't a horrific version of reality in which children are the true soldiers and adults simply copy them. Perhaps it's no surprise that I'm writing this while working on a feature film on child soldiers. The story revolves around a violent and unbelievable encounter in West Africa between UN forces and child soldiers stationed at a checkpoint on a jungle bridge.

Chapter 23: CHATWIN'S RUCKSACK

While I was preparing for Green Ants in Australia, I saw in a newspaper that Bruce Chatwin will be presenting his new book, On the Black Hill, in Sydney. I knew he was remarkable. In Patagonia, as well as his short novel The Viceroy of Ouidah, which follows a Brazilian bandit in West Africa who becomes the greatest slave trader of his time and viceroy of Dahomey. In almost all of my films, I conceived the plot and wrote the script myself, but I had often considered using this novel as the basis for a feature film. I contacted the publisher in Sydney. No, Chatwin was already back in the Outback, researching a new novel.

He launched into one story after another right away—before we had even left the airport—and there followed a breathless marathon of forty-eight hours in which, completely wired, we told each other one story after another, but I had little chance of getting a word in because he talked like a blond. But I believe I was difficult to replace as an opposing number, and we encouraged each other; two-thirds of the time, he spoke practically instinctively, and one-third of the time, I did. Of course, we ate and slept. He got my bed at Paul Cox's residence, while I slept on the sofa. I've heard that on other instances when he was put up by strangers, he would start telling a narrative as soon as he got out of the car and barely acknowledge his host with a nod. He was immediately swamped by people who simply wanted to listen to him. He and I had a beginning I will never forget.

Because I was halfway through my new project, we decided that I would take on his story about the mythical slave trader Francisco Manuel da Silva as soon as the finance was secured. I cautiously asked him if anyone had approached him about optioning the book. Another reason for our direct connection was undoubtedly because we were on foot. Or, more specifically, because we weren't hikers who carried nearly a whole household on their backs in the shape of a tent, a sleeping bag, and cooking equipment, we walked vast distances with little baggage. The world exposes itself to those who go by foot.

Bruce's and my walking style drives us to seek refuge, to put ourselves at the mercy of strangers, because we are completely helpless. I can't recall ever being turned away because there is a profound, even sacred, reflex of hospitality that appears to have been lost in our civilization. However, there were numerous occasions in my life when there was no village, farmhouse, or roof within reach. Then I slept in fields, barns, and beneath bridges, and when it was rainy and freezing and all there was was an empty hunting lodge or remote holiday cottage, I had no issue breaking in. I've regularly broken into locked-up residences without causing any damage since I always take a small "surgeon's kit" with me, which includes a pair of wire rods for opening security locks. I'll leave a letter thanking the owners or finish the crossword problem on the kitchen table.

I invited Bruce to Ghana for the Cobra Verde shoot, but he responded that he was too sick to travel. He had contracted an incredibly unusual fungal infection, which had spread throughout his bone marrow. The mould has only ever been discovered on a whale stranded in the Red Sea and on bats in a cave in Yunnan, China, where he had really been. Later, it was discovered that the mould was a symptom of AIDS. I kept inviting him to visit, and then his condition improved, and he asked if he could come in a wheelchair. For the film, we also hired 800 young women to play the army of Amazons, which were trained on a running track in Accra by the best Italian stunt coordinator, Benito Stefanelli. Stefanelli, who had choreographed innumerable brawls in spaghetti westerns, was confronted with an army of young ladies who were articulate, confident, and nearly hard to control. Bruce witnessed a brief uprising at our Elmina location and writes it in his book with shock. In addition to Kinski, I had an army of magnificent and challenging

Amazons to deal with, and I recall an occasion when the weekly money was scheduled to arrive. After filming, the women changed in our fort's courtyard, and I knew from previous experience that they did not wait patiently in line to be registered and paid. They simply dashed toward the table with the money and documentation, resulting in complete mayhem.

Bruce's condition worsened during the next two years, and I had no idea how sick he was. In 1987, he attended the Wagner festival at Bayreuth, where I was directing Lohengrin. He arrived with his wife, Elizabeth, after driving most of the way on his Citroën 2CV. Next, I shot a documentary film in the southern Sahara about a nomadic tribe called the Wodaabe; there was an annual tribal conference in Niger's semidesert, where there was a kind of marriage market. When Herdsmen of the Sun was finished, I received a call from Elizabeth in Seillans, Provence, where Bruce had retired to an ancient house. He was quite unwell, yet he really wanted to see my film. I got into my car and drove from Munich to see him. I have the film on a videocassette.

When I arrived, Elizabeth stopped me at the entrance and whispered, "Are you sure you want to go in? Bruce is dying." Although this allowed me some time to prepare, I was surprised by what happened next. There was nothing left of Bruce save a bag of bones and those massive eyes blazing from his skull. He could barely speak. He begged to be alone with me. He wanted to see the film right now, so we watched the first fifteen minutes. Then he slipped into oblivion. When he returned, he wanted to see the whole of it, so we watched it all gradually. These were the final sights he saw. His legs—he called them his "boys"; they were now flesh and bone—hurt him, so he begged me to rearrange his guys, which I did. Then he awoke from his semi comatose state and exclaimed, "I have to be on the road again; I have to be on the road again!".

Less than two years after Bruce's death, this knapsack would prove its worth. I had started working on the feature film Scream of Stone. Reinhold Messner had come up with the idea, and the plot revolved around two mountaineers racing up Patagonia's most difficult mountain, Cerro Torre. This mountain resembles a two-kilometre-high granite needle topped by a dome of ice and snow. Only the best mountaineers have been able to make it up there. On an ordinary weekend, twice as many climbers conquer Everest as have ever reached the summit of Cerro Torre. In addition to the smooth, intimidating walls, southern Patagonia experiences incredible storms. Walter Saxer produced and contributed to the screenplay, which later proved problematic because I always prefer to adjust the story to my own point of view. This time, however, I was met with staunch resistance, and I was eventually told that I had to go exactly as per the specified storyboards, which a snowstorm and a cliff face may have different opinions about.

Vittorio Mezzogiorno, the film's lead, wears the leather knapsack as a tribute to Bruce Chatwin. I employed it when it wasn't necessary in a shot. In one scene, once the rivals have reached the dome just below the peak, the younger of the two falls from his harness and is murdered. Stefan Glowacz, a real mountaineer who had gained the title of Rock Master, an unofficial world champion, portrayed the part. Because of storms higher up the mountain, we had shifted some of the shooting down into the valley. For more than a week, we couldn't see or get near the mountain. Then there came a gap. The clouds disappeared, leaving a beautiful, peaceful night filled with stars.

The chopper brought us, the advance guard, up to the ridge about 10 minutes distant. We were placed down, and the helicopter turned away to pick up the safety team. We had only walked a few paces up the ridge; on one side is an Argentine glacier descending from Cerro Torre, and on the other is Chile. On either side, tremendous drops of a thousand metres descend practically vertical granite walls. Then out of the corner of my eye, I noticed something weird. On the Chilean side, far below us, there were rigid small clouds that looked like perfectly still balls of cotton. The air was so pure that you could see them nearly a hundred kilometres distant along the Pacific coast, but now all these white puffy balls were in a hushed commotion. They rose from the depths toward us, resembling nuclear mushroom clouds. I asked Glowacz what he thought was going on, but he just stood there in surprise. I had a walkie-talkie, and I immediately summoned the helicopter. It was only a distant speck by this point, but I saw it turn a circle and fly back to us. When it was almost close enough to touch, the first wave of the storm hit and pushed the helicopter away.

That worried the climbers in the valley. They formed two squads of four to try to get to us via two separate paths. One team quickly gave up in the face of the storm, low visibility, and frigid temperatures. The second got within a few hundred yards of us—vertically—but suddenly the strongest man of them, Argentina's best Andean climber, took off his gloves with his teeth and snapped his fingers to order a coffee. His companions had to rescue him and bring him almost to the glacier before being swept down farther by a little avalanche. There, too, they dug a bivouac and felt safe because they had food, sleeping bags, and a gas cooker to boil snow. Up on the ridge, we forced ourselves to consume snow while keeping our hands and feet moving. We repeated this throughout the next day and night.

Chapter 24: ARLSCHARTE

That worried the climbers in the valley. They formed two squads of four to try to get to us via two separate paths. One team quickly gave up in the face of the storm, low visibility, and frigid temperatures. The second got within a few hundred yards of us—vertically—but suddenly the strongest man of them, Argentina's best Andean climber, took off his gloves with his teeth and snapped his fingers to order a coffee. His companions had to rescue him and bring him almost to the glacier before being swept down farther by a little avalanche. There, too, they dug a bivouac and felt safe because they had food, sleeping bags, and a gas cooker to boil snow. Up on the ridge, we forced ourselves to consume snow while keeping our hands and feet moving. We repeated this throughout the next day and night.

I followed a two-week-old human trail, which eventually came to a standstill. Nobody has been here. Extraordinarily steep slope up multiple snow courses, I noticed a hunting lodge plastered with warning signs, private property guarded by automatic spring weapons. Snow hens fled from me. I could barely see them because, despite the awful weather and dismal sky, I was becoming snow-blind. I didn't have my sunglasses, which was stupid. My eyes were tired and puffy, but I could still see where I was going. My aim at the Arlscharte, the ridgeline, was different in the snow than I had anticipated, but I couldn't miss it for the world. So I spent a long time on a snow mound, thinking over the map and compass.

At the Kölnbreinsperre, the technical team was working on the dam. They'd been there all winter and were still snowed in, isolated from the outside world. They had a telephone and were occasionally delivered food by air. They couldn't believe I'd descended from the Arlscharte. They observed my tracks in the snow with their binoculars and spoke quietly to each other. They assumed I was an escaped criminal. Why had I done this? They wanted to know why

I'd come down that way. I replied that I wanted to notify no one in the world, but I was on my way to propose to my wife, which was best accomplished on foot. The men then showed me their work within the dam. In limitless galleries inside the concrete walls, pendulums were hung, allowing them to read the wall's deformation. Several measurement stations. Dams have extremely complicated inner lives.

Even though he was still in winter, one of the engineers dictated a spring-themed school paper to his daughter over the phone. One man spent hours each day on various training equipment, while another cared for the hotel's hydroponic plants, which he had clustered in the lobby all the way to the offices. I slept on the fourth floor of an empty hotel. I was offered the option of floors. At the end of the day, I strained my ears and believed I heard a distant cuckoo in the valley.

Chapter 25: WIVES, CHILDREN

I had gone hiking to ask for my wife Christine's hand in marriage. The wedding took place in 1986, however despite the dramatic nature of the walk, the marriage did not last. To speak about my spouses would go against my natural prudence; instead, I'd like to remark that all of the ladies in my life were exceptional: gifted, self-motivated, warmhearted, and wise. Christine is a talented musician who comes from a family of music teachers in Carinthia. She debuted as a pianist in a Leonard Bernstein-directed program for young musicians in Budapest when she was fifteen, but at the age of eighteen, she had to give up the piano due to wrist inflammation. She was a political extremist who wrote for magazines. Our kid, Simon, is named after Simon Wiesenthal, with whom she had served. When Simon was bullied by other students at his French lycée and finally told her about it, mother immediately removed him from the school without registering him for another. This was against the law, yet she was unwavering. Simon took English classes for a few weeks in preparation for attending the International School in Vienna. He learned so quickly that he was approved, and within a half-year, he had passed all of the intermediate stages and was placed alongside "native speakers." All of my children's success can be attributed to their mothers, not to me.

I met Martje, my first wife, on the cruise to the United States. She was also musical; she played the harpsichord and continues to sing in choirs, notably Bach's choral music. Her real interest, however, is books. She came from a teaching family and grew up in Dithmarschen, in northern Germany, with four sisters in a female-dominated environment. We got married after she finished her studies in Freiburg. She appeared in almost all of my early films, including Signs of Life and Even Dwarfs Started Small, and on Aguirre, she did the most unappreciated task of all: administering our practically nonexistent cash in the jungle. I've never heard her complain about it. According to the macho role-playing of the time, she was always more of my guardian than I was of her. When I unexpectedly decided to travel to the Caribbean in 1977 to make La Soufrière, a film about the volcanic eruption, I stopped at home for a few minutes to get my passport. There was our tiny boy, and it was far from certain that I would return alive. I bring it up because this is not the type of behaviour that a marriage can endure. But almost without recognizing it, we were growing apart.

Eva Mattes and I had a daughter named Hanna-Marie. Eva wanted the name Marie to connect to her role in my film Woyzeck, for which she won Best Actress at Cannes. It was an injustice that Klaus Kinski did not receive the Best Actor award, and Eva treated him as kindly as he did her. I never meant to have an intimate relationship with any of my actresses, but I fell madly in love with Eva while we were simultaneously working on Stroszek in 1975. Some things are self-evident, yet they grow clearer when spoken aloud. Recently, she has turned her attention to written materials. I'm quite wondering what she'll do next. She has Eva's warmheartedness, and her voice and giggle are so close to her mother's that I've occasionally addressed her as Eva on the phone.

At Chez Panisse, a Bay Area restaurant, I met my wife Lena, whom I've now been married to for twenty-five years, thanks to Tom Luddy. I owe Tom a lot. Really, he should be designated as a national cultural treasure of the United States. As a young theoretical physicist, he studied under the famed Edward Teller at Berkeley, where he became a leader in the Free Speech Movement. At the same time, he was a junior amateur golf champion and might have pursued a professional career. His revolution-minded classmates at Berkeley, however, ridiculed him for it, calling golf a bourgeois activity, and Tom gave it up. He oversaw the Pacific Film Archive in Berkeley, which became the most important film culture institution on the West Coast. Errol Morris and Les Blank, both directors, were present.

A pair of young women were waiting at the bar because our table hadn't yet arrived. One of them turned to face me; it was Lena. Apparently, while I don't remember it, I remained glued to the spot at the top of the steps, captivated by a bolt of lightning. I'd never seen eyes with such beauty and intelligence in my life. That evening, I picked a free chair and sat between her and her neighbour, and we talked for the entire supper as if there were no one else around. I discovered that during her school days in Siberia, she had secretly duplicated by hand a couple of novels that were banned in the Soviet Union and distributed them among trustworthy acquaintances. She had reproduced the entirety of Bulgakov's The Master and Margarita and Solzhenitsyn's first novel, One Day in the Life of Ivan Denisovich. The evening was unparalleled. I knew immediately that this was the woman I wanted to live with.

Only this time, I wanted to do everything right. I returned to Vienna, where I was still formally married but had already split. I organised my house and gave away everything I owned. I returned to the United States with no luggage, nothing at all. I desired a fresh start. I had already gone through passport control and customs when the official called back to ask where my luggage was. Had I forgotten something on the carousel? It made me appear suspect; if I'd had a bomb on me, I could have left it running around on the conveyor belt. I explained that I had come without anything. The official informed me that in twenty-two years, he had never seen somebody arrive from another continent without luggage; at the very least, they would have had a carry-on or a briefcase. I pulled my toothbrush from my jacket pocket out of sheer foolishness, most likely to impress him.

Only this time, I wanted to do everything right. I returned to Vienna, where I was still formally married but had already split. I organised my house and gave away everything I owned. I returned to the

United States with no luggage, nothing at all. I desired a fresh start. I had already gone through passport control and customs when the official called back to ask where my luggage was. Had I forgotten something on the carousel? It made me appear suspect; if I'd had a bomb on me, I could have left it running around on the conveyor belt. I explained that I had come without anything. The official informed me that in twenty-two years, he had never seen somebody arrive from another continent without luggage; at the very least, they would have had a carry-on or a briefcase. I pulled my toothbrush from my jacket pocket out of sheer foolishness, most likely to impress him.

Working our way up the Pacaás Novos was challenging because the river is scarcely accessible even for small boats, with too many fallen trees blocking the waterway. After extensive preparations, we met the first two war chieftains who had survived the initial meeting, Tari and Wapu, outside their reservation. In addition to six-foot-long bows and arrows, like those used by the Amahuacas on the Fitzcarraldo shoot, they now used shotguns and requested that we provide them with one and ammo. We complied and traded them for some of their arrows. One of them is the ending of 1971's Land of Silence and Darkness, without a doubt my most profound film. When a farmer becomes deaf and blind and is no longer acknowledged by his family, he spends years in his cowshed with the cows for animal warmth before abruptly rising from a park bench and walking into the boughs of an October apple tree. The deaf and blind man's sensation of the twigs followed by the trunk of the tree is difficult to express. In Ten Thousand Years Older, Tari observes a giant ticking kitchen alarm clock that we brought with us. His expression and the clock—if I'd only videotaped that moment in my life, it would have been worthwhile.

The best moments were always when I was filming and Lena was working on a picture project at the same time. On Wheel of Time, my 2003 film with the Dalai Lama, she collaborated with me on a book project titled Pilgrims. I frequently carry her big cameras, some of which are specifically designed for large-format celluloid prints. When we circumambulated the sacred mountain of Kailash in Tibet with a hundred thousand pilgrims, she had altitude sickness at around 5,000 metres. Our yak, which had been brought along by two of our guides to carry luggage, immediately dropped its burdens and stampeded off into freedom. Our guides were subsequently pushed to their limits by the weight of food and a tent, and when Lena could no longer put her feet in front of each other, I took her knapsack along with mine. We had various projects on the table-top mountains on the border of Venezuela and Brazil; we were in Mexico; and we were in Japan for the opera Chūsingura, where Lena met Hiroo Onoda, the Japanese soldier who only surrendered twenty-nine years after the conclusion of WWII. He concluded that the war was still ongoing based on numerous clues; only later did he realise that Korea and Vietnam were America's successor conflicts. In 2022, I wrote a short novel about him called The Twilight World. Lena and I worked together on Cave of Forgotten Dreams in the Chauvet Cave in the Ardèche area of France, Invincible in the Baltics, Queen of the Desert in Morocco, and Salt and Fire in Bolivia's Uyuni salt flats. Lena photographed the production shots for my most recent feature film, Family Romance, LLC, which was shot in Japan, and meeting Gorbachev was particularly memorable because we were both in Russia. We don't speak German or Russian with each other since it works out better for us to meet on a plane that isn't entirely hers or mine. It makes us both cautious in a language that neither of us originally spoke.

Chapter 26: WAITING FOR THE BARBARIANS

For a feature film project based on J. M. Coetzee's novel Waiting for the Barbarians, we scouted locations in Kashgar, Xinjiang, China. We then travelled to the mountains near Pakistan, Afghanistan, Kyrgyzstan, and Uzbekistan. I wanted to look further into the Hindu Kush and the northern Pamirs. In Tajikistan, I once played a zealous prophet in Peter Fleischmann's science fiction film Hard to Be a God (1989), who is brutally executed with a spear after twenty minutes. I instantly developed a rapport with Coetzee, but the film's financing never came together. Since then, everything about Kashgar and the Uyghur situation has deteriorated dramatically, but there was still a weekly market visited by 200,000 Uyghurs from all over. It was like a thousand years ago on the Silk Road, with bearded guys speaking Turkic and Muslims wearing long robes and fur hats. I recall one little portion of the bustling market where around three thousand men were selling nothing but roosters; each man had one under his arm. I recall a truly awful traffic congestion of eight hundred donkey carts, everything entangled with everything else, and the donkeys braying. I recall how, as if on cue, a crowd dispersed, a long path opened up, and a magnificent horse galloped in my direction, ridden by a barefoot six-year-old without a saddle. The horse rose up in front of me, as if responding to a phantom phenomena, turned on its rear hooves, and galloped away. The roadway closed up like a sea once it had been divided. The horse was purchased on the spot. For my film My Son, My Son, What Have Ye Done?, I returned to Kashgar for a dream sequence starring Lena and Michael Shannon. In a dream, Michael's character finds himself hopelessly lost in a weird prior existence. He passes through a crowded livestock market, and everyone stops to stare at him, as if he were an apparition from another realm. We attached a big wooden breastplate to Michael's upper body and set three arm-length tripod legs on it, radiating out from him. There was a camera focused on his face. As he moved through the crowd, I was certain that everyone he passed would turn to look at him. Michael agreed to the improvised scene at the foreign place as long as I stayed with him at all times. Michael didn't want to be detained on his own because we didn't have a work visa or permission to film, which we had little hope of receiving given the political atmosphere there, but he did want to be arrested with me if we had to. It sounded like a reasonable wish to me.

Lena deserves credit for encouraging me to bring out the diaries I kept during Fitzcarraldo. In multiple notebooks, my script, which is usually regular size, became smaller and smaller, until becoming minuscule. It can now only be read using a jeweller's eyepiece. I also wanted to preserve some distance from this difficult period in my life. Four or five years after the events of 1979 and 1981, I opened my records and transcribed about thirty pages of them, but it was agonising to confront everything again, and I was confident I would never touch it again. More than two decades later, however, Lena told me that it was time to reconsider those notes since they did exist; otherwise, some idiot would get to work on them when I was no longer present. After some hesitation, I decided to try looking at them again, and it was suddenly easy. Everything that had been upsetting and burdensome had vanished. That helped to shape my book Conquest of the Useless. Similarly, many years later, and at Lena's insistence, I revisited my notes from my discussions with Hiroo Onoda. This gave me The Twilight World. What I'm writing today stems from Lena's encouragement. Lena, who was in the room with me, inquired what it was about and reminded me that I was working on a number of projects that were neither films nor books, but rather a type of "interzone" between the two. She was correct, and I called Whitney back the next day.

Chapter 27: UNREALIZED PROJECTS

The "interzone" continues. In 1976, I filmed a film on the world championship of cattle auctioneers called How Much Wood Would a Woodchuck Chuck, which was inspired by my fascination with language's limits. That is why Hölderlin and the Baroque poet Quirinus Kuhlmann are so significant to me, because they both pushed the boundaries of my own language, German. When Stroszek's ambition of moving to America is dashed, his mobile home is auctioned off. The performer in the sequence was a former world champion livestock auctioneer whom I tracked down in Wyoming and persuaded to come out of retirement for the film. His auction, in which language becomes singsong, a cascade of craziness that cannot be intensified any further, will undoubtedly leave an impression on anybody who watches the video. I've always suspected that this screaming was the final form of poetry, or at least the last language of capitalism. I've always wanted to direct a Hamlet with all of the roles played by ex-champion livestock auctioneers, and I wanted the performance to be less than fourteen minutes. Shakespeare's text is already well-known, and an audience would only have needed to refresh their minds quickly to prepare for the presentation.

When I was living in Vienna, I believe it was in 1992, the Wiener Staatsoper approached me to see if I wanted to direct an opera. I replied that I'd much rather write one myself; I already had most of the music and would only need to come up with the lyrics. That piqued many people's interest. I had a long talk with their dramaturg, whom I'll simply refer to as B. here. My plan was to construct an opera based on Gesualdo, with the majority of the music drawn from his sixth book of madrigals. As Prince of Venosa, Carlo Gesualdo (1566–1613) was independently wealthy, therefore he was able to write without being dependent on the church or benefactors. His music is typical of the late Renaissance period, yet in his sixth book of madrigals, he writes music as if all of his circuits had blown. These types of sounds were only heard again three centuries later, in the late nineteenth century, and it's no coincidence that Igor Stravinsky, who was heavily influenced by him, made two pilgrimages to Castle Gesualdo near Naples. He produced madrigals for Monumentum pro Gesualdo, a memorial to his predecessor, which premiered in 1960. Later, it was transformed into a ballet.

I also had plans to conduct Wagner's Götterdämmerung at one specific location, Sciacca on Sicily's south coast. This location is unknown to most people, and it is rarely mentioned. Sciacca was formerly a Carthaginian, possibly even Greek, settlement; the small town of 40,000 people is otherwise quite unremarkable. But it does have an opera house. I don't have any evidence, but I've always assumed that the opera house was built solely to launder Mafia money, because it never opened and had no director, administration, program, stagehands or electricians, chorus, orchestra, singers, or anything else. I wanted the opera house to serve its purpose, even only once. I would have hired an orchestra, chorus, soloists, lighting engineers, stage designers, and the works. Before the third act, I would have cleared the premises and moved the audience and actors to a safe distance before blowing up the opera. We would have concluded the piece with the smoking wreckage. The local government was not opposed to my concept because the opera was an eyesore in the first place, and I had already contacted the best demolition firm in America, which was based in New Jersey. All I knew about the building were images and architectural blueprints, but when I arrived in Sciacca to begin construction, it was evident that the concept was impracticable. The modernist pile was reinforced concrete and would have required a considerable amount of dynamite, and just next to the opera, with shrubbery growing from it, is a massive hospital that would have either gone up or been severely damaged.

Because I've recently been attacked by insanely politically correct people who question why I would direct Wagner in the first place, I've prepared a series of responses. The first one is a question: why did Daniel Barenboim conduct Wagner, particularly in Israel? Without a doubt, Wagner's personal nature is terrible, and he was an antisemite. But he is not responsible for Hitler or the Holocaust, any more than Karl Marx was for Stalin. Wagner's music is irresistible. Similar issues about guilt and universal condemnation arose regarding Kinski after his daughter Pola revealed in a book that she had continued incest with her father. Pola, like a number of other young women, had approached me for advice and support before publishing her book. I have no doubts about her account.

I wanted to create and execute an oratorio and ballet for elves in Alaska's North Pole. The North Pole is home to Santa Claus and his reindeer. Hundreds of thousands of messages addressed to him are mailed from the United States and elsewhere. The majority of them convey regular infantile wants, but every now and again one stands out. I've read several of them. A youngster wishes her father would stop abusing her mother and allow her to get out of her wheelchair. There is a large group of elves who answer letters on Santa's behalf. The top children from the local middle school are chosen for elf duty, and the strange thing is that a massacre was planned by this same bunch of elves. At least six children, none older than fourteen, had already equipped themselves with their fathers' rifles and handguns; the date had been set; and the list of potential victims had been circulated to staff and students. Following their actions, the elves planned to block the railway line that runs through the North Pole with tree branches before boarding a freight train bound for Fairbanks. They hadn't noticed that these tracks had been inactive for a year. Then they wanted to go out into the world with new names like Luke Skywalker and Darth Vader. On the eve of the coup against Santa and everything associated with him through sentimental impulses, one of the mothers discovered information of the plan on her son's computer, and the plan was dismantled. All of the conspirators were ejected, but there were no further legal ramifications. In the North Pole, I was met with a wall of quiet. Under threat of legal action, I was denied access to everyone involved in the conspiracy; the police became interested in my visa; and the school even threatened me. I was compelled to admit that there was nothing happening here.

Erik Nelson had placed me on the trail. He is the producer with whom I collaborated on Grizzly Man in 2005, as well as films on the Antarctic and Chauvet Cave. He was also the one who encouraged me to begin work on Into the Abyss right away, despite the fact that there was no outline or funding for it, but the impending execution of the murderer Michael Perry made no room for delay. Through that video and eight others about death row inmates, I saw deep into an abyss.

I met Erik at a tiny environmental film festival in Wyoming. He approached me and immediately assisted me in securing money, as well as introducing me to a network official from the Japanese broadcaster NHK who was also present. This happened while I was preparing for the film The White Diamond, which was about an airship in the jungles of Guyana. When I returned to Los Angeles, I paid Erik a visit at his Burbank production company to express my gratitude for his selflessness. When I stood up to leave, I realised I had dropped my vehicle keys and scanned a low glass coffee table piled high with papers, DVDs, and an old half-eaten salad on a plastic plate. Erik, assuming one of the papers had captured my attention, handed me an article. "Here, read through this. We're planning something interesting in Alaska." Then, back at home, I read one of the first pieces about Timothy Treadwell, who had spent many years living with wild grizzly bears in Alaska, convinced that he needed to defend them from poachers. In his time in the wilderness, he had, almost in a Walt Disney Esque sense, overstepped a limit: he got too near to the bears, stroked their faces, sang to them, and told them how much he loved them. He had gathered videos of remarkable quality and beauty over the period of eleven years, but one summer, he and his partner were ambushed and eaten by a grizzly bear. I suddenly had to make a film. The sense of urgency drove me back to Erik Nelson. I asked him how far along they were with the project and heard that they will begin filming in less than ten days since the late summer salmon migration in Alaska had begun, which is when grizzly bears congregate on riverbanks to catch fish. I posed the question, "Who's directing?" Erik looked at me and responded, with scarcely a pause, "I am, kind of." I heard the word "kind of." I could tell he was unsure of himself. I looked at him and answered, with all the authority and assurance of my long-gone religious period, "No." "I am going to direct this film." I extended my hand, and he shook it impulsively, perhaps out of relief. A few days later, I arrived in Alaska.

After Grizzly Man, there were several additional films featuring Erik Nelson, the intellectual and complex figure that he is. After our nine videos from death rows in Texas and Florida, there were supposed to be four more on the same subject, but the last one refused to let me leave. It was about a young man who, during an unsuccessful drug-induced exorcism, murdered a little girl who had only recently learned to walk and talk. Although I had ordered the local homicide detectives to show me only images of the crime scene, not the body, they inadvertently projected the little girl's body onto the screen. I've seen some truly horrific things. I've never been frightened to look into an abyss, but I wouldn't want my worst enemy to see what I saw back then. As I prepared to make more death row films, I was awakened in the middle of the night by a scream. Lena beside me awoke promptly; she, too, had heard the scream. That was my own scream. At that point, I knew I had to conclude the series and leave the subject at that. It is possible to have one's own emotional household.

On October 9, 1963, a tragedy happened, killing around 2,400 people. The dam is one of the world's tallest structures, standing at 262 metres. It plugs a narrow gorge. In the fervour for industry and technology that typified Northern Italy in the 1950s, they did not want to hear about the obvious risk associated with such a project. The Monte Toc slopes on the reservoir's south side were exceptionally steep and unstable. A geologist was frightened, but he was removed, and the Italian government even tried a number of critical journalists on charges of "undermining public order." Fifty million cubic metres of water poured over the top of the dam, which had to withstand the landslide, and cascaded down the gorge in an unfathomable deluge. After a few kilometres, the tsunami crossed the Piave Valley and accelerated up the other slope to the small village of Longarone. Longarone was completely destroyed. There were over 2,000 dead. The cold water caused several of the victims to have heart attacks. According to an Italian Catholic newspaper, this was a trial sent to us by God out of love.

I wish to make a film about the poet Quirinus Kuhlmann, whom I have already discussed. He was a poet and religious zealot who walked around Europe in the second half of the seventeenth century, preaching and battling with other mystics. He came from Silesia and sought to usher in a new spiritual era, for which Kuhlmann produced Der Kühlpsalter. He was preoccupied with alchemy, and because he took everything literally, he set out to find the stone of wisdom armed with a shovel. Filled with holy zeal, he embarked on the last known crusade with two ladies, a mother and her half-grown daughter. He proceeded to Constantinople to convert the sultan, but by the time they arrived in Genoa, the women had had enough of him and fled with a group of sailors. Kuhlmann almost perished while swimming after the ship. He arrived in Constantinople, and while attempting to contact Sultan Mehmed IV, he was seized and imprisoned. However, from prison, we have his Kühlpsalm 14.

I'd like to do a film with Mike Tyson about the early Frankish kings. He and I met when a Hollywood producer wanted to film a documentary about him. There were production representatives there, as well as five lawyers. Tyson was understandably nervous, so I convinced him to walk out on the balcony. When we spoke alone, man to man, we immediately hit it off. Instead of chatting about the film, we discussed his childhood. He grew up in a single little room with his mother. He was frequently present when there were gentlemen calling and snatched money from their empty trousers. By the age of twelve, he'd been arrested forty times. When he reached the age of legal accountability, he learnt to box while in juvenile jail and became the world's youngest heavyweight champion ever. Later, after being sentenced to six years in prison for rape, which he fiercely rejects, he began reading voraciously. He is familiar with the Roman Republic, the early Frankish dynasty of the Merovingians (Clovis, Childeric, Childebert, Fredegund), and Carolingian Pepin the Short. Tyson had quickly squandered $300 million after the conclusion of his boxing career and was sitting on a massive mountain of debt; thus, I presume, his financial demands of the production firm were so outrageous that the film could not be made.

I will never catch up with me. Another unfinished film about someone who vanishes or becomes invisible. I've had several chats with Kevin Mitnick, maybe the best hacker of all time, who was able to evade the FBI for a long time before being arrested and serving five years in federal prison. There is a video about the early Irish monarch Sweeney, who becomes lighter and lighter after a major fight until he can fly, then rests in a tree and begins singing like a bird. No one can take him down. He eventually dies of weariness after assisting a monk in pulling a large turnip from the earth. Sweeney Among the Nightingales is a children's film. But this inability to keep up does not make me breathless; I accept it.

Chapter 28: THE TRUTH OF THE OCEAN

In the maze of recollections, I frequently question myself how much is in flux, what was important when, and how much has gone or changed tone. How accurate are our memories? The question of truth has troubled me throughout my works. Today, it is even more urgent for all of us since we leave traces on the internet that have a life of their own. The issue of false news has gained widespread attention due to its significant impact on political life. However, falsifications have existed since the advent of written signs. In reliefs, an Egyptian pharaoh celebrates his tremendous victory over the Hittites, yet a written record of the peace treaty that was signed indicates that the war was indecisive. We had phoney Neros, who appeared in northern Greece and Asia Minor with large retinues following the death of the Roman emperor. We have the fronts of Potemkin villages designed to impress Catherine the Great as she travelled down the Dnieper. It's an endless list.

I was confronted with facts from the beginning of my work. You have to take them seriously because they have normative force, but I've never been interested in making just factual films. Truth does not have to coincide with facts. Otherwise, the Manhattan phone book would be titled The Book of Books. Four million entries, all factually valid and subject to confirmation. But that tells us nothing about any of the dozens of James Millers in there. His number and address are correct.

My film Lessons of Darkness, depicting the blazing oil wells in Kuwait at the end of the Gulf War, opens with a quote from Pascal: "The collapse of the stellar universe will occur, like creation, in grandiose splendour." The film is not a political statement about Saddam Hussein's withdrawing Iraqi army; you could see and hear that in primitive form every night for a year on the television news. I was thinking of something different. When I landed in Kuwait, I sensed that something bigger was going on: a cosmic event, a crime against creation. Throughout the film, which feels like a requiem, there isn't a single shot in which we can recognize our planet. The film is presented as a science fiction apocalypse. Hence the Pascal before the opening scenes—I wanted to boost the viewer's level and hold him there till the conclusion. But the quote is not from Blaise Pascal, the French philosopher who left us with magnificent aphorisms about the universe; it was written by me. I believe Pascal could not have phrased it better. Another thing: in such cases, I always made it clear that I was making things up.

I'm constantly amazed by how individuals understand the "truth." In the Fitzcarraldo shoots, the commune of the local Machiguenga tribe deep in the jungle requested cash payment in exchange for their participation, as well as a permanent medical outpost, a transport boat, and our support in their efforts to obtain title to their land, or territory. We first hired a surveyor to create a map with borderlines, and then, with two Shivan Korean officials, we visited Peru's president, which resulted in the acceptance of their territorial rights a few years later. There was a moment in Lima when I realised "the truth of the ocean." In the Machiguenga village, there was a debate about whether there was an ocean and whether it contained salt water. When we were with them, the two Machiguenga representatives waded out into the surf, completely naked, till the water reached their armpits and they tasted the water all around. They then filled a bottle with seawater, sealed it, and carefully transported it back to the forest. Their proof was that if there was salt in one region of the sea, all of the water in it would be salty, just like in a giant cauldron.

Chapter 29: HYPNOSIS

After being forced to give my own commentary on ski jumper Steiner and appear in the film as the chronicler of his life, I realised there was a positive aspect to this assignment, which I had initially rejected. Speaking one's own words has an authentic and unique quality that any audience would recognize and that no trained actor or professional speaker can equal. I fell into this role without much consideration, but I didn't want to come across as inexperienced, so I worked hard for precision and effect. Another aspect was that I was unsure how to depict a full village sleepwalking into a completely predicted disaster in my feature film Heart of Glass. The film's topic is a real person, a cowherd in the Bayerischer Wald in the late eighteenth century who had the gift of foresight and, like Nostradamus, saw a world on fire and the end of humanity. The community survives on glassmaking, but the glassblowers have lost the secret to manufacturing ruby glass. He was technically competent at his profession, but when people come up with this sort of New Age nonsense, I become irritated. I took on the role of the hypnotist; I had done my research and was conversant with the literature. The self-important New Ager later established an institute that specialised in hypnotising young women and sent them to ancient Egypt as temple dancers. They then spoke what he said was the pharaohs' language, but Egyptologists listened and confirmed that it was just meaningless sounds with no connection to any known language. In reality, anyone can hypnotise. The mystifications stem from our lack of understanding of the mechanics of the brain switching off during hypnosis and sleep. All we actually know is that we must proceed methodically. There are basic approaches, such as fixing the subject's eyes with the point of a pencil. This is followed by a particularly intense and intriguing manner of speaking.

There are some prerequisites for hypnosis. The person must have provided their consent and be willing to follow the instructions. If a person lacks the imagination and mental flexibility required to follow recommendations, hypnosis becomes extremely difficult, if not impossible. Very old people, with fixed thinking, are difficult to mesmerise. Small children, such as four-year-olds, who are full of energy and have short attention spans, are also difficult to hypnotise—and should definitely not be attempted. One has no influence over entranced individuals. Murder under hypnosis occurs only in terrible films and literature since it has no effect on our fundamental nature. If you offer a hypnotic individual a knife and instruct them to kill their mother, they will simply reject. Subjects are still capable of lying. As a result, evidence obtained through hypnosis is not admissible in court. It is also critical to gradually restore the subject's normal consciousness so that they can reenter the world free of dread and with joyous expectation. But I, too, was expecting some surprises. When one musician responded to a newspaper advertisement and showed up for a test, he was a little nervous. All of the invitees understood they were there for a test and that I was putting together a company of actors, so the young man asked if he could bring his girlfriend. I positioned her in the back of the room as an observer and instructed her not to follow my vocal cues. However, after a few minutes, she was the first to go into hypnosis. There was also an incident during filming in which one of the actors was so complacent with his situation that he refused to follow my directions and come around step by step. It took a long time to wake him up. Decades later, in my film Invincible, the pianist Anna Gourari, who played the female lead alongside the world's strongest man, voiced severe qualms about being hypnotised on camera. We had a few witnesses, and she fell into such a profound trance that it took me a long time to awaken her.

Chapter 30: VILLAINS

Soon after my first few films, I was requested to stand in front of the camera as an actor. The initial offer came from Edgar Reitz, a founder member of the New German Cinema who had previously helped me personally. He and Alexander Kluge, who headed a film school in Ulm, had invited me there early on; I suppose they were both confident that whatever it was, I had it. I turned them down. I was always an autodidact; I didn't believe in universities. But both directors provided me useful advice for my own shows, and what truly was important was obtaining a steady supply of partners from them. I hired Beate Mainka-Jellinghaus, who had previously served as my editor. Beate has an incredible aptitude for movies; she recognized, almost instantly, what we would find valuable. She handled me harshly, almost pitilessly. On my first film, Signs of Life, we were supposed to look at a six-hundred-yard loop of footage, but it turned out to be reversed. She inserted the film nevertheless and viewed everything in reverse at five times the speed. She threw the entire twelve-minute roll away after it had rattled through. Later, Harmony Korine and David Lynch ranked the picture among their favorites.

At the time, everything was on celluloid. Analog sound was recorded and then transferred to broad, uncomfortable cassettes with perforated edges that allowed sound and picture to be synced, similar to film tapes. Edgar Reitz had a sound machine approximately the size of a gym locker and let me use it for free in his production suite. In the late 1960s, he began filming a series of short films called Stories of the Dumpster Kid, in which he cast me as a mad murderer. I did fairly well, and from that point forward, I was given an endless supply of crazy and villain roles. But there were a few outliers.

In 1989, I appeared in Peter Fleischmann's science fiction film Hard to Be a God, which was based on a classic novel by the Strugatsky brothers. I played a zealous, prophetic preacher who is quickly dismissed by the ambitious forces that be. A spear strikes me from behind, killing me. A stuntman pushed the spear into a plank of wood strapped to my back, although he appeared reluctant. Both Fleischmann and I thought it didn't look like much, so I encouraged my killer to be more enthusiastic. I had no idea he was a former Soviet middleweight boxing champion. The second time, the jolt he gave me knocked two crowns off my teeth. We shot in Kyiv, Ukraine, in a large studio from the golden period of Soviet cinema, and on location in Tajikistan's Pamir highlands. My work on that picture is one of my few direct contributions to New German Cinema. I don't think I fit into that group. My films were always something different.

Technically, my first appearance comes at the opening of Signs of Life, when the wounded main character, Stroszek, is taken out of an army truck and treated in a village. The extra I had engaged did not appear, so in an emergency and because it did not fit anybody else, I put on the uniform. Today, I'm amazed to see myself as little more than a schoolboy. Much later, I played myself in Zak Penn's 2004 film, Incident at Loch Ness. I portray a director who is compelled to compromise by an unscrupulous producer (Zak Penn)—even at gunpoint if necessary. The gun is only a signal flare pistol, not really usable for anything other than threatening someone, but the whole thing appears so convincing that a big portion of the audience believed it was real and was on my side, despite the fact that it should have been obvious from the start that it was all a setup. What I did in the film was pure self-irony. Moments like that have always been beneficial for me. However, because the whole sense of context has been lost—what is satire, what is make-believe, and what isn't— a large portion of the audience was unaware that what they were watching was planned and directed. The film is an early take on fake news, which currently dominates the media.

In 2008, I appeared in another Zak Penn picture, The Grand, which he wrote and directed. The setting is a casino in Las Vegas during a poker tournament, and I play "the German," who cheats and is eventually sent out. "The German" is a pitiful character who carries his pet rabbit everywhere while also wishing to strangle other small animals in their cages to remind himself of his own existence. For the record, there is no aspect of my character that would lead a writer to develop such a role for me. It is pure creation on Zak's side, and hence pure performance on mine.

I had expected Harmony Korine's style to be totally guerrilla, but working on his project exposed some of the things that hold the film industry in a viselike grip. The team, all young and passionate people eager to be a part of something completely new, fled in panic when a picture was removed from the wall and a dozen or more cockroaches beetled away from behind it. They were only willing to return to work once the production team provided everyone with hazmat suits that resembled those used to clean up nuclear sites. Harmony and his videographer then ostentatiously removed practically all of their clothing and continued to work in their Speedos. Harmony informed me that he bought them on this occasion. Another thing that surprised me was the abundance of phones and walkie-talkies in the very confined space of the house; team members standing almost next to each other would only speak via their phones.

My black humour was more well accepted in the United States than in other countries. So it came as no surprise to me in 2002 when Matt Groening, the creator of The Simpsons, contacted me to see whether I'd be interested in playing a cameo part on the show. To begin with, I wasn't certain. I assumed I'd seen printed versions of The Simpsons as a comic strip in newspapers, but I was mistaken; there was no printed version. But I'd never seen them as animated cartoons on television before. Matt Groening laughed down the phone at me, claiming that The Simpsons had been famous for twenty years. He thought I was kidding when I requested him to let me watch one of the recent episodes on DVD so I could hear the cartoon voices and practise my own version. But all he needed was my native English voice; that would be enough to make him happy. He may not have said it directly, but that is what I understood him to be saying.

My black humour was more well accepted in the United States than in other countries. So it came as no surprise to me in 2002 when Matt Groening, the creator of The Simpsons, contacted me to see whether I'd be interested in playing a cameo part on the show. To begin with, I wasn't certain. I assumed I'd seen printed versions of The Simpsons as a comic strip in newspapers, but I was mistaken; there was no printed version. But I'd never seen them as animated cartoons on television before. Matt Groening laughed down the phone at me, claiming that The Simpsons had been famous for twenty years. He thought I was kidding when I requested him to let me watch one of the recent episodes on DVD so I could hear the cartoon voices and practise my own version. But all he needed was my native English voice; that would be enough to make him happy. He may not have said it directly, but that is what I understood him to be saying.

The director Jon Favreau approached me to appear in the Star Wars spinoff The Mandalorian. He is a big fan of my films, and when I told him I hadn't watched any of them, he promised to help me get to know the Star Wars universe. He showed me some very spectacular costumes, sample storyboards, and models of exotic worlds. In the series, new technology with spherical horizons would be used, eliminating the need for green screens, which were essential in all prior fantasy and science fiction films. The actors can see the planet they are travelling on or the spaceship that is transporting them all around them, and the camera can see everything. You don't have to appear to be under dragon attack while standing in front of a green screen. The cinema has returned to its original and proper place.

The level of secrecy surrounding The Mandalorian was

unprecedented. I was hired to create phoney trails for a Huckleberry Finn film. You were not allowed to leave the studio during filming, even for lunch, unless you covered your costume entirely with a long tunic. A security guard at the gate checked you out. Fans were lurking outside, having managed to sneak onto the lot to take shots with their smartphones. The popularity of these films and the expectations of a global community are astounding. When the veil of secrecy was finally lifted at the premiere, I said something about the mechanical Baby Yoda, which sparked ten million comments on the internet within an hour.

Chapter 31: THE TRANSFORMATION OF THE WORLD INTO MUSIC

I was drawn to opera in the same way as I was to acting. It wasn't just the result of my picture Fitzcarraldo, which was about bringing grand opera to the jungle; it was more about the usage of music in all of my films. Music is never just background in my films; it enhances the imagery and creates even more striking visions. In 1985, the director of Bologna's Teatro Comunale approached me about a production of Ferruccio Busoni's Doktor Faust. The opera was left unfinished since the composer died before completing the score, and the libretto is completely disorganised; the entire composition is considered unperformable. My brother Lucki, on the other hand, encouraged me and had a knowledgeable agent, Walter Beloch, on his side. Together, they persuaded me to visit Bologna's opera house.

Although I can barely read music, I felt fully confident in this new position from the start. I went to my first opera staging at La Scala in Milan; I had no notion what operas looked like or what the current trends were. Because I was so unfamiliar with the opera world, my personal creation stood out from anything else on stage. My work was to begin with Doctor Faust, who had been lost in his studies; for this, I asked my set designer, Henning von Gierke, to build a rock face leaping up into the sky against some low-lying clouds. Henning was originally a painter, but he has worked on a number of my films, creating magnificent backdrops for Nosferatu, Fitzcarraldo, and others.

The music, as with all of my productions, was the driving force. I realised that when the entire world is converted into music, the result is opera. And I realised that the heightened emotional world of opera is completely unique; it does not exist in human life or in nature. Opera compresses and intensifies feelings, but they are real to the audience because of the strength of the music. Feelings in grand opera are like principles of feelings, or mathematical axioms, incapable of further reduction, concentration, or explanation.

I've directed operas by Verdi, Bellini, Wagner, Mozart, and Beethoven. Spending a short amount of time working with music, breathing music, and translating a world into music has always helped me feel grounded. Opera, however, requires a separate technique. The world of opera is made up of manufactured elements, including dramas, intrigues, and scandals. Everything is, in fact, pretty safe—the music has been written, the buildings are strong and well-roofed; unlike filming in the forest, there's no risk of a storm catching you off guard. The entire orchestra, including the singers, knows the piece by heart. However, unless there is a mysterious sense of impending doom and mystery, the entire situation can become lifeless. Your production has died. I believe that the perpetual dread of controversy stems from the singers' profound worries of being pushed out on stage and having to strike exactly the proper notes with split-second timing. There is no second chance, and the audience, barely dimly visible in the half-light, is a relic of the old gladiatorial arenas. They want to see blood. I was at La Scala and witnessed the best baritone in the world being relentlessly booed in the middle of an aria due to minor vocal issues.

During rehearsals, I developed the practice of causing some movement or disruption when it appeared that everything was going too smoothly—without the spark, fire, gossip, scandal, or danger. Il Guarany, starring Placido Domingo, was directed by me in Washington, DC in 1996. He asked me to conduct an almost forgotten opera by a nineteenth-century Brazilian composer. The rehearsals went well; everyone sang the correct notes, but something didn't click. I decided to spread a fake tale about Placido Domingo's day off. I gently asked someone in the administration if she had notified the cast that Placido would be unable to attend the premiere due to an obligation at the Met. It only took a few moments for the place to go crazy; the singers were chatting, and then there was music again. Without these contrived dramas, the premiere and future performances will fail. Adrenaline-producing events must alleviate the underlying fear.

A bomb threat was issued during the dress rehearsal of Wagner's Tannhäuser in Palermo, forcing the theatre to be evacuated. (This time, it wasn't my fault.) The production was nearly entirely irrelevant because Tannhäuser has essentially no storyline, simply souls in turmoil. There was hardly any set. All of the effects were the result of light and air, which were moved by precisely regulated ventilators. I paired it with extremely light garments created from a special parachute silk and developed by my buddy, the brilliant costume designer Franz Blumauer, so they fluttered with the slightest gust of wind, like spirits made apparent. In dramatic moments, ventilators concealed in thirty locations were activated, and the enormous veils flapped in intense distress. I remember how, after the theatre was vacated, all of the singers and Venus, who was wearing a great crimson veil, went around Palermo's deserted streets.

Chapter 32: ON READING MINDS

I visited a temporary nuclear holding facility in New Mexico, where radioactive barrels are held in massive salt mines. Locals are overwhelmingly opposed to the initiative, despite the fact that the mines are deep down and have not changed geologically in 250 million years. The question is, how can we warn future generations not to enter the mine? In a few thousand years, no one will speak or understand our languages in their current form. It's even possible that all of our languages will disappear. In a section on a preventive medicine campaign in Uganda from my 1969 film, The Flying Doctors of East Africa, I demonstrated how the residents of a rural village were bewildered by the posters used. They had no newspapers, books, or television. Curious, I questioned what they saw on the public health poster of an enormous eye, and the responses ranged from a rising sun to a large fish, despite the fact that the preceding image was meant to illustrate how to protect the eye from infection. Finally, I displayed four of the photographs used in the educational campaign side by side, one of which was purposefully hung upside down.

I've always been curious about how images of the far future are created. Even if we have to picture a future without a script or any grasp of historical links, I can imagine a time scale of forty thousand years, which is the gap between the Chauvet Cave and the present. Books will be gone; the internet and constellations will have changed; the Big Dipper will be much longer. Someone had the idea of turning the cactus cobalt blue through genetic mutation as a kind of nuclear threat warning for the New Mexico nuclear dump, but it's just as probable that they would have spread over North and South America or gone extinct entirely due to climate change.

To me, understanding Linear B is one of our most significant cultural and intellectual achievements. Initially, no one understood what language the signs were written in, although there were examples of words or sign combinations with varied endings that suggested an Indo-European language. Despite the fact that we do not know the language, we can sound out Etruscan using its Latin-based alphabet. Etruscan is most likely a non-Indo-European language that we will never grasp unless we come across a Rosetta Stone. Linear B contains more than seventy different signs, indicating a syllabic script. In addition, there are other ideograms, such as a jug for "jug" and a vehicle on wheels for "cart." Number indications in the decimal system were quickly identified. Two problems remained unanswered: what sounds were produced by the various syllabic signs, and what language were the tablets inscribed in? Michael Ventris, an architect and classicist who worked on cracking German Luftwaffe codes during World War II, used logical grids that grew more complete over time, and John Chadwick, a classicist and expert in early Ancient Greek dialects, came to the compelling conclusion that it had to be an archaic form of Ancient Greek that was perhaps current seven or eight hundred years before Homer.

Chapter 33: SLOW READER, LONG SLEEPER

I live in Los Angeles. Lena and I had to determine where we'd reside in the United States, and the decision was obvious right away: in the city with the greatest substance. LA is identified with the glitz and glamour of Hollywood, but it is also the birthplace of the internet, and all of the major painters, writers, singers, and mathematicians have relocated here from New York. The influx of Mexicans has immensely energised writing and music. Electric cars are being designed here, while reusable rockets are being built in the city's southern outskirts. Pasadena, approximately north of Los Angeles, serves as the mission control hub for several space enterprises. A lot of mundane occurrences originate here as well: aerobic studios, inline skating, strange sects. I could go on.

I'm a slow reader because I frequently stop reading to imagine scenes and circumstances before returning to the words on the page. Some works, such as Thomas Bernhard's Walking, took me two weeks to read past the first paragraph. That book's opening sentences are so wonderful that I never stopped being amazed. I can actually only read while lying down. That is most likely due to the fact that when I was growing up with my mother and brothers, there was never enough space at the table for me to read, but there was plenty of room on the floor with my head on a cushion. I work quickly, without endless retakes. My shooting days normally end at 3 or 4 p.m., though I may go until 6 p.m. I can't recall ever doing overtime. I strongly despise night shoots because I am not a night owl. I write my screenplays once I have the full film in front of me, and it rarely takes me more than a week to finish one.

I avoid interacting with fans. I occasionally watch garbage TV because I believe the poet should not avert his gaze. I'm curious about what others aspire to. I'm a good but restricted cook. My steaks are outstanding, but they will never compare to what you can find on any street corner in Argentina. Tree huggers seem suspect to me. Yoga lessons for five-year-olds, which exist in California, strike me as strange. I do not use social media. If you find my profile anywhere there, you may be certain it is a forgery. I do not use a smartphone. I don't trust the media, so I obtain a more accurate view of the current situation by consulting numerous sources—the Western media, Al Jazeera, Russian TV, and, on occasion, downloading an entire politician's speech. I trust the Oxford English Dictionary, which is one of humanity's greatest cultural achievements.

Anderson and Dibble, the English translators, were outstanding scholars at the University of Utah. Utah is a research centre for pre-Hispanic culture because Mormons think the Aztecs are one of Israel's lost tribes. Their text is as powerful and authoritative as the King James Bible. At the time, I had an unfinanceable project about the conquest of Mexico from the perspective of the Aztecs, for which I had studied the fundamentals of classical Nahuatl with a grammar book and a dictionary. I made a trip to Salt Lake City to see Charles Dibble, who was then eighty-four and retired. Professor Anderson was already dead. Dibble, a nice, calm, profound gentleman, was shocked to be contacted by a German filmmaker who admired his work. After thirty years of work, the University of Utah Press released a twelve-volume bilingual Nahuatl and English edition of the Florentine Codex. We became friends throughout our one long day together, but we never saw each other again. Charles Dibble died shortly after we met.

Chapter 34: FRIENDS

I have few pals. You could certainly consider me a loner. It's difficult to keep in touch with folks since we live so far apart: Wolfgang von Ungern-Sternberg in Regensburg, Joe Koechlin in Lima, Uli Bergfelder in Italy, and Berlin. Uli created the ideas for me across many years and films; he assisted with the superstructure of the ship in Fitzcarraldo and was frequently an advance scout—for example, in Australia for Where the Green Ants Dream. On-site, he could always repair anything with an excellent touch. He occasionally travelled for me, such as to Kazakhstan's Aral Sea, where ships rust in the sand that was once the seabed. We had examined it as a viable setting for Salt and Fire (2016), but after receiving his report, I abandoned the idea and instead filmed at Bolivia's Uyuni salt flats. Uli specialises in Provençal poetry, yet he lives on an old agricultural estate in Volterra with nine hundred olive trees. He spent years restoring a collapsing farmhouse ruin. Being with him was always enjoyable and stress-free. He has a cameo appearance in Nosferatu. When the ghost ship from the Black Sea arrives at Wismar, full of rats, he is the sailor who frees the dead captain, who has bound himself to the wheel with rope.

Herb Golder and Tom Luddy, film editor Joe Bini, cameraman Peter Zeitlinger and his wife Silvia, my fellow directors Terrence Malick, Joshua Oppenheimer, and Ramin Bahrani, all of whom live far away, and Angelo Garro, who lives a little closer in San Francisco, are also among my pals. Angelo is a Sicilian blacksmith who established his own forge in San Francisco, but he is also a person from another era—he is a hunter and gatherer who produces his own wine, olive oil, pasta, prosciutto, and sausage. Once or twice a year, he will hunt a wild boar and roast it over coals in his forge. He prepares his own flavoured salt and Sicilian sauces using his grandmother's traditions. I collaborated with him on a short film for a Kickstarter campaign, which was really successful. Every important American cook has visited him in his forge, and I don't know any of them who do not admire him. Everything about him is right, proper, and necessary.

Werner Janoud is one of my close buddies. Because he and I have the same first name, he now goes as Janoud. Janoud was poor in the Vogtland of the former German Democratic Republic, without his father, who had vanished in Stalingrad, and began working as a tungsten miner at the age of 14. Conditions were terribly harsh, and when he was nineteen, he attempted to flee to the West. He was hauled off the S-Bahn bound for West Berlin after making himself suspicious by carrying all of his documents with him. They took away his passport. A few days later, he managed to depart, this time using his twin brother's passport. In Cologne, he worked in a steel rolling mill as well as a jam factory. But he wanted to be out in the world. He soon collected enough money to purchase a bicycle and travel to Montreal by ship. He had a companion with him, but he left after a few days. Janoud rode a bicycle across North America to the Pacific. On the way, he worked as a farmhand and learned English through discussions. He was not an alphabet, and he could read well, but he still struggles to write. He then travelled south alone, via the United States, Mexico, and Central America, where he acquired Spanish and began photographing. His photographs from that time have a stunning depth, and because he was unaware of any trends, they have a unique expressiveness. After three and a half years on the road, he settled in Lima and worked as a photographer for local newspapers. I met him through soccer manager Rudi Gutendorf, who trained five teams in the early days of the Bundesliga before becoming a globetrotter working with various national teams throughout the world. When I was in Lima for Aguirre's preparations, I would participate in the fitness training of his squad, Sporting Cristal Lima. When the A squad faced the B team, they were without a player, so Gutendorf assigned me to the B team. Which position did I wish to play? I stated I didn't care, but I wanted to compete against Alberto Gallardo. Gallardo was the Peruvian international winger chosen by journalists for a World Eleven alongside Pelé and other legends after the 1970 World Cup in Mexico. Gallardo was a speed freak, a madman who performed insane things on the field and never delivered what you anticipated. I wanted to make things difficult for him, or at least get in his way, so I feverishly tried to follow him about. After ten minutes, someone handed the ball to me, and at that point, I had forgotten which team's shirt I was wearing and which direction we were playing, and after fifteen minutes, I slunk off the pitch with stomach cramps and vomited for hours into the oleander bushes beside it. Janoud pulled me out of the shrubbery, and we became friends right away. In Aguirre, you can see him in the raft, spinning around in the rapids until Aguirre smashes it with a cannon. Janoud is utterly primal and self-made, and he is the only person I know who has not been distorted by human society.

Janoud was also connected to Fitzcarraldo. While the team was filming elsewhere, he and a girlfriend remained at the forest camp to prevent the locals from dismantling it for building materials. The first time around, he impressed Mick Jagger since his experience was so unlike everybody else's, and hence his viewpoint on life was unique. He had not heard of the Rolling Stones. He kept asking Mick what his name was, and Mick patiently tried to correct him. "It is not Nick. It's M, as in mother.' Milk." But Janoud couldn't get it right, saying, "Oh, right, Nick, as in 'pain in the nick.'" Then Janoud would laugh like a donkey, and Mick Jagger would follow suit. Janoud inquired whether Nick earned money from his singing and if he would mind picking him a melody on his guitar. Mick did so without hesitation, using his electric guitar and amp just for Janoud. Later, Janoud departed Peru for Munich. Before moving to America, he and I shared a leased property in Pasing, near Munich. He was a wonderful buddy for my young son Rudolph. Years later, to commemorate Rudolph's coming of age, the three of us travelled to Alaska and landed in a small seaplane on a lake west of a mountain range. We didn't have a tent, so we created our own shelter. We had an axe, a chainsaw, hammocks, a rubber dinghy, and fishing rods. We had carried some basic supplies with us—rice, noodles, onions, salt, and tea—because the nearest settlement was four hundred kilometres distant. We wouldn't have gone hungry, but we had to find our own berries, mushrooms, and fish. After six weeks, the jet came to fetch us up. It was such an amazing experience that we repeated it the next year on a different lake. Janoud paid me a visit in 1994, when I directed Bellini's Norma at the Verona Arena. His Peruvian girlfriend was working in Bologna at the time, so he travelled from there to see me. He appeared depressed and withdrawn for a few days, so I finally asked what was up. Janoud was devastated when he discovered his girlfriend was pregnant. It was early, and we were in a café near the arena. I summoned the waiter and requested a bottle of champagne. How fantastic; he would be a father; there could not be finer news—I congratulated him, and we drank to it, and Janoud was overjoyed at the thought. He married his fiancée, Rosa, and their daughter, Gretel, is now an adult and independent.

Chapter 34: MY OLD MOTHER

In the last six years of her life, my mother studied Turkish from a female friend in Munich who was from eastern Turkey. My mother paid her a visit there, travelling alone in rattletrap buses across Eastern Anatolia with live lambs among the passengers. Her health gradually deteriorated over the years. At the very end, I had to travel to the United States because producer Dino De Laurentiis had planned a large film project with me. I told my mother, "I will not go. "I am staying here." She answered, "You should go; you must go. "Life must live." I flew to New York, where I found that she had died overnight. I spent time with my friend Amos Vogel, who had cancelled all of his plans for that day. He spent the entire day with me in solitude and prayer. That night, I flew back.

Chapter 36: THE END OF IMAGES

I envisage a world without novels like this one. People have ceased reading for decades, and university students are no exception. This development is the consequence of tweets, text messages, and short films. What would the world be like with few spoken languages, which are becoming extinct in their abundance and variety? What would the world look like without a meaningful visual language, where my career no longer exists? The end is approaching. I envision a fundamental shift away from cognition, reasoning, and image, not just an approaching darkness in which certain items can still be felt, but a state in which they no longer exist at all, a darkness filled with horror and imaginary creatures. I recall a line in the Florentine Codex written as if its people, despite the devastation of their culture and horizons, were still attempting to find their way to their language: "A cave is dreadful, a place of terror, a place of death. It will be known as a location of death because people will die there. It is a place of gloom, perpetual darkness. It stands there with its mouth wide open." How does one express the absence of images? Not simply their elimination, the last, irreversible turn away from images, but their nonexistence? I imagine two mirrors put up in complete opposition, reflecting nothing but themselves into infinity. But there's nothing for them to mirror. If the mirrors were one-way mirrors, such as those used by detectives during interrogations, the opposite mirror would display a void. There is no criminal confession, no table, chair, or lamp, only empty space that is repeatedly reflected. Nothing else, no life, no breath. No Frenchman is eating his bike. There was no second Frenchman who switched into reverse and drove his antique automobile backward into the Sahara. No truth, no falsehood. There is no river known as the River of Lies, Yuyapichis, which masquerades as the much bigger Pichis River. No Japanese marriage agency would request a bucketful of sand to be discharged from a satellite so the bride may be surprised by a shower of meteorites. No more twins living in separate bodies but thinking and speaking together. There were no parrots during Alexander von Humboldt's 1802 voyage up the Orinoco, where he came upon a town whose entire population had been eradicated by a plague. Their language had perished with them, but for the previous forty years, the adjacent community had cared after their parrot. This parrot still spoke sixty different words in the dead village's tongue. Humboldt jotted them down in his notebook. What if we taught those words to two parrots and they could communicate in them? What if we project ourselves far into the future and picture objects we've built that will continue to exist for, say, two hundred thousand years? A period when humanity will very surely be extinct, but certain of our monuments may still exist, indestructible. The dam in the Vajont gorge resisted a massive landslide of 250 million cubic metres of rocks, earth, and gravel. At its base, this dam is twenty-eight metres thick and made of particularly hardened concrete. This lower half would almost definitely remain, standing majestically without conveying any message to anyone. There would be a crystal pure trickle of water from the rocks to the side, sought for by herds of deer, as though

The contents of this book may not be copied, reproduced or transmitted without the express written permission of the author or publisher. Under no circumstances will the publisher or author be responsible or liable for any damages, compensation or monetary loss arising from the information contained in this book, whether directly or indirectly. .

Disclaimer Notice:

Although the author and publisher have made every effort to ensure the accuracy and completeness of the content, they do not, however, make any representations or warranties as to the accuracy, completeness, or reliability of the content. , suitability or availability of the information, products, services or related graphics contained in the book for any purpose. Readers are solely responsible for their use of the information contained in this book

Every effort has been made to make this book possible. If any omission or error has occurred unintentionally, the author and publisher will be happy to acknowledge it in upcoming versions.

Copyright © 2023

All rights reserved.

Printed in Dunstable, United Kingdom

65428358R00077